HORIZONS
NEW VEGAN CUISINE

Rich Landau & Kate Jacoby

Book Publishing Company
Summertown, Tennessee

Bundt pan is a registered trademark of Nordic Ware. Grand Marnier is a registered trademark of Marnier-Lapostolle. Grey Poupon is a registered trademark of Kraft Foods. Old Bay Seasoning is a registered trademark of McCormick & Company. Pernod is a trademark of Pernod Ricard New Zealand Limited. Vegenaise is a registered trademark of Follow Your Heart's Natural Foods Market and Cafe.

ISBN 978-0-615-16126-6 (acid-free paper)
Printed in Hong Kong
18 17 16 15 14 13 12 11 10   2 3 4 5 6 7 8 9

Book Publishing Company
PO Box 99
Summertown, TN 38483
88-260-8458
www.bookpubco.com

Library of Congress
Cataloguing-in-Publication Data
Landau, Richard S.
Jacoby, Mary Katherine
  Horizons: New Vegan Cuisine / Rich Landau & Kate Jacoby
      p. cm.
Library of Congress Catalog Card Number:

Photography and book design by Donna Gentile Wierzbowski of DG Design & Photography. Cover design by John Wincek.

In loving memory of Kate's dad,
Theodore E. Jacoby

CONTENTS

ACKNOWLEDGMENTS

After almost 14 years of business, we know that Horizons would not be where it is right now without some very important people. We'd like to offer the most heartfelt thanks to a few of them…

Our Families. You're incredibly understanding of our hectic schedule, and we really appreciate your efforts to schedule all get-togethers on Sundays so that we can always join in. Thanks especially to Suzanne for finding the time to give her professional assistance whenever possible.

Our Amazing Staff at Horizons. We have been fortunate enough to work alongside some truly great people on this journey. There must be something about working in a vegan restaurant that builds extra commitment and dedication, and we thank you for making this restaurant a diamond in the rough. Especially in the kitchen, where our current crew (Ross, Mark, Leah, Michael, and Allison) has made this job the most enjoyable it's ever been! Special thanks to Ross for his 5+ years of commitment, enthusiasm, and loyalty. And particular thanks go to Rachel Klein and everyone who helped test recipes for this book.

Chris. We would have never opened if it wasn't for your generosity, time, and support. It will never be forgotten.

The Press. We know that you're just doing your jobs, but the end result has been so overwhelmingly positive for us. Best yet, you have made "vegan in Philly" a hot topic, and we are eternally grateful for the buzz! Thanks especially to Joy Manning and *Philadelphia Style Magazine* who believed in us enough to feature a vegan chef on the cover alongside the other heavy hitters in town!

Oz. Every chef dreams of a produce guy like you—the man who will track you down on the street, slam on his brakes, and cut across traffic so he can give you the first bag of mousseron mushrooms in town. You are an invaluable resource and a great friend.

Our Customers. Your comments, praise, encouragement, and gratitude have been overwhelming. Thank you for choosing to spend your hard-earned money and your precious time here with us for a meal.

And once again…Donna. You are an inspiration—the perfect balance between best friend and drill sergeant! It was just what we needed to make this second book a reality. Thanks for all your hard work, creative energy, and support! ▪

FOREWORD

By Michael Klein, *Philadelphia Inquirer*

I wish someone could bottle Rich Landau and Kate Jacoby's passion for cooking and for life.

When I first met Rich more than a decade ago, he had just opened a lunch counter in a hippy-dippy health-food store near Willow Grove Park mall. The burbs. A land that had seldom seen bean sprouts outside of a Chinese restaurant and where tofu was that square stuff in plastic packages that nobody bought.

My daughter, who had announced a few years before at age 5 that she "would not eat anything that has a face," inspired me to drop in. She loved it—what does a kid know, right? So did I. Rich was on to something. We followed him to nicer digs next door when he moved out of the health-food store (and wisely found Kate), and we now applaud their move to the big-time—Center City Philadelphia, near the bustling South Street corridor.

Rich and Kate are no longer the big fish—well, maybe the big tofu—in a small pond. Within a few blocks of Horizons are dozens of Philadelphia's most popular restaurants. Horizons stands right up there, drawing praise from critics and the public.

Too often, critics will damn a vegetarian restaurant with the faint praise, "Even carnivores will like this place." That's unfair. Rich and Kate simply adhere to creative, uncompromising cooking; the fact that it's vegan is a plus.

And it's thriving in a meat-centric city like Philadelphia—where the annual chicken-wing-eating contest gets international coverage and the passion for cheesesteaks runs to the bone.

Every city needs a serious vegetarian restaurant, just as it needs stellar examples of other cuisines. Horizons completes us. Where's that dress-up place to take cousin Karlene, visiting from Minneapolis, who subsists largely on noodles and cheese-less pizza? Where does a vegan couple go for a stylish night out, complete with drinks? (Yes, Horizons is the rare veg restaurant that has a liquor license.) Or how about a meatless business meeting? I planned to interview Dan Mathews, the globe-trotting rabble-rouser from PETA. Seeking a place where he'd feel comfortable, I called Rich and Kate, who whipped up a meal that Dan's still talking about, starting with the rolls and finishing with the crème brûlée.

I was proud to take him to Horizons, Philadelphia's destination vegan restaurant. ▪

HORIZONS IS A PEAK EXPERIENCE

By Vance Lehmkuhl, *Philadelphia Daily News*

If that sounds like trumped-up marketing-department hyperbole, don't worry, I hear exactly what you're saying.

You're saying you haven't been to Horizons yet.

Well, it's worth the trip, to put it mildly. And yes, I mean from wherever you are right now, assuming you're somewhere in the Western hemisphere. If you've been to Horizons, you know: It's not just a great vegan restaurant, it's a great restaurant. More than that, it's just a great time. From when you come in the door to when you amble contentedly back out onto Seventh Street, you're engulfed in a world of scintillating comfort. In short, the Horizons experience is what Philly's renowned ultra-posh dining rooms wish they could engender—and that's no exaggeration.

I'm referring specifically to the Horizons now operating in downtown Philadelphia, but the restaurant was already something special in the years before 2006, when it was Horizons Café in the northern suburbs.

I remember one day at the *Daily News* when I was chatting with gossip columnist Dan Gross about vegetarianism, he said, "You been to that place Horizons Café out in Willow Grove?" Well, I had heard of it but hadn't been there—I pictured a curbside window with a couple picnic tables on the sidewalk or something, juices, smoothies— maybe worth swinging by sometime if I happened to be up that way.

Dan said it was worth a trip of its own, just for the Barbecued Seitan Wings. He raved about this appetizer to the point that I went out to Willow Grove to check it out, and damn if he wasn't right (so let me pause here to say, officially, thank you, Dan). But it was more than the wings. Horizons "Cafe" was an honest-to-god fine-dining restaurant with a serious but relaxed ambiance, and there was an attention to the look of the food, the textures, the smells, the general presentation, that primed you to savor every bite.

I wrote up the seitan wings in my vegetarian food column in the *Daily News* and made the trek to Willow Grove a once-a-season highlight with my family. Soon they moved a couple doors down and reopened with a new look, vibrantly colorful, brighter and more diner-like. But the quality of the food didn't change—excepting, perhaps, that as chef Rich Landau got more confident in his abilities, the combinations and juxtapositions of ingredients and flavors became more daring and more rewarding. The fruits of his and Kate Jacoby's trips to the Caribbean, his dishes often took on a tropical cast, sometimes with an east-Asian overlay.

The Pan-Seared Tofu, Pacific Rim Grilled Tofu, and Grilled Seitan Steak became favorites with my family, though the one inviolable constant was the seitan "wings" as appetizer to every meal. Meanwhile, the desserts, which started out with optional vegan varieties, went all-vegan; Kate Jacoby became pastry chef and mastered dairy- and eggless dessert creation.

Around this time I persuaded the *Daily News'* restaurant critic to try the place. While she was "impressed" by the "great flavors" and the "fabulous cook" behind them, she lamented that Rich was wasting his talents on "mock meats" instead of "the real thing." Rhetorically, she asked, "Why not just establish a cuisine entirely independent of meat, not one constantly referring to it?"

It's a no-win cliché of veggie-dining critiques that if a cuisine lacks a meat-like protein source, that's a fatal flaw, but if there is something meatlike, then the cry is, "Why are meat-shunning vegetarians still "aping" meat dishes?" I thought it was kind of lame to haul out that chestnut in the review, but maybe Rich took it to heart. When Horizons relocated to Philly last year (sans "Café"), all the animal references were dropped: The "wings" are barbecued seitan, plain and simple.

Of course the move downtown brought other changes—a more upscale dining environment, an even classier organization of waitstaff, a melt-in-your-mouth complimentary focaccia—but with the shedding of meat-analog terms, Horizons' cuisine has moved to a new level. Diners now experience Rich's one-of-a-kind creations without a preconceived filter, and in plate after plate, that experience is superlative. True, it's still food for thought: "I eat there and I think: Why do I need to eat meat, again?" as one omnivore friend put it. But Horizons lately has transcended vegetarian advocacy, putting all its customers back in touch with how simply, utterly delicious food can be.

This book is part of that effort. Horizons' first cookbook came out in 2003. Even since that time, Rich and Kate have paid more visits to tropical climes and learned more about getting the "flavors of the sun" into their cooking. This new offering reflects that intensification of Rich's quest to bring out the best and brightest in his ingredients, and with practice it may rub off on you.

Now, of course these recipes are not going to make all your home-cooked dishes taste just like Horizons, nor will all your meals become peak experiences—there's too much of Rich's personality in what he delivers to tables night after night. But they will familiarize you, in a hands-on way, with Rich's vision of cooking. And whether you hit it on the head or not, you will wind up with delicious, nutritious, fascinating vegan food.

Again, if you are in or around Philadelphia or can reasonably get there, you owe it to yourself to experience Horizons first-hand. But either way, this cookbook will give you more than a taste of the culinary philosophy behind a restaurant that merits consideration as Philadelphia's best. ∎

INTRODUCTION

Years ago, I was on the French island of Guadeloupe, reading menus and deciding on where to eat dinner. I walked into this beautiful looking place and started talking to the owner, who spoke English and seemed to be a really nice guy. "Sure, we can accommodate a vegetarian, no problem," he said. "We will make you a special vegetarian entrée." His charm had won my vote on where to eat that night.

Later on that night when I returned, the place was jumping, and the guy who I had spoken to earlier that day was insane—he was the only one working the floor in this huge restaurant. Standing at the door, we made eye contact, and I gave him a "remember me?" smile, expecting a knowing wink back with the promise of a vegetarian Caribbean extravaganza he had in store for me. Not so, he just shrugged off my greeting and then ignored me. Bad sign.

When I was seated and he asked for my order, I gave another knowing smile: *Don't you remember this afternoon? I'm the guy you are going to dazzle with some blow-my-mind French tropical cuisine?* No, he didn't remember me. Another bad sign.

So I ask him what on his menu is vegetarian. He replied, "We don't cook vegetarian." My instincts tell me to leave, my stomach tells me to stay and try to find something to eat. So I order a dish that I recall as a vegan nightmare. A sort of loose quiche with eggs and cream, baked in a gratin dish. It came with a beautiful ground thyme sauce on top that I will never forget, but the rest of the dish was disgusting.

While this is going on, I watch him deliver two steaks to the table next to me. I eavesdrop on his delivery, "We serve only local vegetables," he says to the guests, and there on these plates were five or six small piles of different vegetables and starches that he was explaining to the customers. And I'm thinking, why couldn't he just have given me those vegetables, I would have been ecstatic—French Caribbean vegetables in the French Caribbean!!! This isn't happening!!

But if you are vegan or vegetarian, this story probably sounds all too familiar. It is the story of our lives, and it usually gets worse.

But don't worry, that's why we made Horizons. So that we can have a place to celebrate food and a place to prove to the carnivores that we are not crazy.

So before we officially start this new cookbook, let's back up just a bit as to how we got here.

Where's the Beef? … Really.

There is no doubt that most of you, like me, grew up with animal protein as the centerpiece of your meals. I mean, how many American families of the '50s '60s or '70s would actually have a meal of just green beans and rice? Or carrots and potatoes? Back then, your neighbors would have labeled you a communist or hippie. Nowadays, well, you're a vegan, and a struggling one at that! It's not easy at first to satisfy your craving for protein and to ease that inner nagging from your childhood that you have given up something. We've been there and done that. We have suffered for too long on pasta and salad, and we're fed up with lentil loaf and steamed broccoli. We are tired of people leaving things out of our meal so that we can have a veg-plate.

I don't see why if you have gone vegetarian that you should be deprived of, shall we say, paella (as an example). Are we supposed to just eat a bowl of saffron rice with peas in it? That's a nice side dish, but let's not be silly here. Vegetarians need a meal like anyone else. When we decided to go vegetarian in the first place, we decided to abstain from eating animal flesh. We did not pledge to give up sustenance and hearty satisfaction when we dine. We don't want half portions; we don't want side dishes. We want food like the carnivores. We don't want to be punished for our sacrifice.

That's where the Horizons system kicks in. The goal of our restaurant and our cookbooks is to show people that you can still be a gastronome, a foodie, passionate about cooking and eating, and all the while, not eating animal meat—yet still being truly satisfied. We want to offer you too many reasons not to have to go back to meat. So in this book, you will find many recipes for people who do not want to change their lives just because they are cutting something out of their diet. This is the good stuff, this is the food Kate and I love to eat, the food that keeps us happy and healthy. This is the food that we serve at the restaurant, for company, and in our home. I hope this book is a source of satisfaction and celebration for you.

As with our last book, we are not trying to show off or offer you fantasy visions of food that you will never attempt to make. We are not trying to intimidate or impress you. We want you to be happy, and we want your life to be easy. It's a meal—a beautiful thing—but it's not astrophysics.

In this new book, you will find a lot of tropical influence. Some are ideas from our travels, some are new inspirations from the now easily accessible variety of ethnic markets within walking distance of us, and some are right off of our menus. And again we have tried to make it so that these recipes are a source of fun and inspiration for you and not just formulas to follow.

Remember to buy quality ingredients. In the long run they are actually cheaper.

Remember to cook with spirit, not method. Don't follow a recipe—cook it!

Remember to taste and enjoy. Don't just eat.

And finally … just to catch you up from where we left off in the last book, we have since moved Horizons to downtown Philadelphia, where we occupy a beautiful new building. We purposely limited the seating so that we could provide a quality experience for each guest. The focus is on the dining experience here, not on high volume. It is the way quality food should be enjoyed.

The press has been unbelievably kind to us with our move. The upscale vegan dining experience is something that Philadelphia has been lacking for some time. Our biggest triumph was finally receiving a "3 bell" review from restaurant critic Craig LaBan. Read his reviews or his book and look at some of the company we have in that category. It is truly an honor and a great day indeed for the credibility of vegetarianism.

And on Sunday, September 5, 2004, I officially became the luckiest man in the world when Kate and I got married by the water's edge at Lake Nockamixon.

And we are far from done.

Rich Landau
Flying home from somewhere warm
01/30/2007

IN YOUR KITCHEN

For those of you who are new to meatless cooking, we recommend that you read this section in its entirety to get acquainted with the cooking techniques, terminology, and recommended spices. For those of you who have been vegetarian for a while, we hope that you will find a new, interesting, or easier way to prepare your favorite food. You will also find secrets, tips, and special touches that we use at the restaurant.

We've separated this cookbook into seven main sections and an index. Use this section as your springboard to creative cooking. Taking a few minutes now to review the information will help you get things underway quickly. We've included over 80 new recipes within these pages, from an appetizer like Vietnamese Bruschetta to a decadent ending, like the Chocolate Peanut Butter Bomb, and every dish and condiment in between.

Remember to have fun and always be willing to experiment. No recipe ever comes out exactly the same way twice, so enjoy yourself!

Working with Tofu

Tofu has, unfortunately, become the evil icon of vegetarianism. It seems tofu is responsible for turning so many people off and giving the whole vegetarian thing a bad rep. It's been my life's work to make tofu palatable. I have to say, I love the stuff, but it took me years to learn how to prepare it properly.

So what is tofu? Tofu is a soy-bean-curd cake. Very simply, soybeans are boiled, a coagulating agent called *nigari* is added, and a curd comes to the surface, almost like a cheese. It's then skimmed off and pressed into bricks. Kate and I had the pleasure of visiting the "Fresh Tofu" kitchen (Fresh Tofu, Inc.) in Allentown, Pennsylvania. We drove up expecting to smell the incense, part the beads, and see a few hippies laboring away while listening to the "Dead." What we found instead was an ultra modern, Willy Wonka-esque machine-world fantasy land. It really impressed us how far this has all come.

So, how did I find tofu? Well maybe like the rest of you, I first tried it in a bad Chinese restaurant and spit it right out. It reminded me of when I would chew my eraser in second grade. Subsequently, I shunned it for years.

As my culinary explorations continued and I gained more confidence, I tried embracing tofu for what it is. Rather than follow the already navigated paths of throwing small pieces of tofu into a big stir fry to try to "absorb" the rest of the flavors around it, I decided to focus on the tofu. Low and behold, tofu actually can taste good! Fresh, quality tofu cooked through the center, with a golden crust, has convinced many of our customers that tofu is a pleasure for vegetarians and meat eaters alike.

My favorite two ways to prepare tofu are to pan-sear it with a spice crust or to grill it after marinating it for hours. We will go into detail for both of these methods on the next two pages, as well as several alternative preparations that we also use at the restaurant. Tofu will keep for more than a week if you ensure that it is completely covered in water and that you change the water at least every other day. When you are ready to use it, leave it out on the counter to let some of the water drain out. You also can press it under a book or frying pan to make it denser if you like, but that little bit of extra water remaining inside can make tofu nice and juicy. It's up to you.

PAN-SEARED TOFU

This is the restaurant's signature way of cooking tofu. With minimal oil, the result—once mastered—is a wonderful golden crust that is full of flavor. The keys are salt and pepper here. Use whole spices, grind them separately in a coffee mill until they are coarse, and then mix them together. Use whatever supporting spices you like or those that you have available. Here is a basic recipe to get you started.

Tofu Spice

2 tablespoons coarse salt
2 tablespoons peppercorns, black or mixed
1 teaspoon coriander seeds
1 teaspoon caraway seeds
1 teaspoon fennel seeds
1 teaspoon cumin seeds
1 teaspoon celery seeds (do not grind)

Directions

1. Liberally coat a 1-inch slice of tofu with the tofu spice on one side.
2. Place a shallow layer of canola or olive oil in a sauté pan.
3. Heat until very hot (you'll see slight ripples, but don't let it smoke).
4. Turn off the heat and gently lay in the tofu, spice side down.
5. Return to heat, spice the other side, and cook until the bottom looks golden.
6. Turn off the heat and carefully flip it with tongs or a spatula.
7. Turn the heat back on and cook the other side until golden brown.

Note: When done properly, most of the oil should still be in the pan.

GRILLED TOFU

This is a simple technique to impart flavor into your tofu dish. The marinade is for one pound of tofu cut into three slabs.

Basic Marinade

½ cup olive oil
¼ cup tamari soy sauce
1 tablespoon black pepper

For variations, add mustard, BBQ sauce, Latin Spice, or Island Spice (see the *Common Ingredients for Savory Foods* section that follows for the spice blend recipe).

Directions

1. Let the tofu sit in the marinade for at least 20 to 30 minutes.
2. On a hot grill with very clean grates, gently lay the tofu slabs down and leave them for about 3 minutes.
3. Turn the tofu one-quarter turn to create crisscrossed grill marks and cook another 2 minutes.
4. Brush the top of the tofu with the marinade and flip it.
5. Brush the already grilled side (now face up) with the marinade again and let it sit for 3 to 4 minutes.

Working with Seitan

Seitan, more than anything else, is what brings customers into Horizons. Seitan is a lot easier to prepare than tofu, and you could practically eat it right out of the package if you so wanted. It takes on meat-like textures and flavors that make it such a convenient steppingstone into meatless cuisine. Essentially, seitan is wheat gluten. All flour is made up of starch and gluten. By washing all the starch out of your flour, you are left with just gluten, which is then simmered in a flavorful stock to become seitan.

Seitan is a super food. It's practically fat free, very low in carbohydrates, and loaded with protein. It also does a marvelous job of substituting the hearty, meaty protein portions for which many vegetarians long and to which meat eaters are so accustomed.

Here are some basic tips that you should always follow when working with seitan. The first thing you want to do when you buy it is drain and wash off the liquid in which it was packed. If you don't use it all right away, try a new recipe the next night; it perishes rapidly. I've included recipes within this cookbook that are opportune ways to use up all the little bits and scraps that you will accumulate when using seitan. You can also freeze all the little bits and then take them out to use when you have enough to make one of the "scrap" recipes. Seitan scraps are also terrific in spaghetti sauce, sloppy joes, and tacos.

Working with Tempeh

If you thought tofu was tough to get the hang of, then you are in for a challenge when you get to tempeh. Tempeh is a fermented soybean cake. Unlike tofu (the soybean curd), tempeh actually contains the whole soy bean. It's dense in texture, but has a very interesting flavor that takes well to Asian and Indian preparations because of its nuttiness.

More often than not, I've seen vegetarian restaurants choose to sandwich tempeh with layers of sauces and condiments to make BLTs or Reubens. That's good stuff, but Kate and members of my kitchen staff have convinced me over the years to continue working with tempeh, to highlight its unique qualities rather than cover them up. Now I'm really proud of the tempeh dishes that we serve at the restaurant.

Tempeh really needs to be braised or steamed first to open it up a bit, and then it can really take on some flavor. After that, tempeh can be pan-roasted, baked, and, best of all, fried.

18

Basic Cooking Methods & Techniques

Whether you plan to make tofu, seitan, mushrooms, vegetables, or a whole meal, below are some basic cooking methods that you will use when preparing the savory recipes found within this cookbook. For cooking methods regarding baked goods, refer to the *Desserts & Baked Goods* section for more information.

Grilling

This is my all-time favorite preparation method with the jumping flames, the char marks on juicy zucchini or meaty mushrooms, the smoky essences on tomatoes and Belgian endive—and, oh—the peppers and onions!

To grill, you need just a little oil. Most of it burns off, and you're left with wonderful flavor. The type of grill you use makes a big difference. If you are using an outdoor BBQ grill, the racks tend to be high up off the flames, and the marks you get may not be very defined. I like to keep my outdoor grill on very high heat, allowing it to heat for about 10 minutes before putting anything on it. If some of you are lucky enough to have an indoor grill, you will notice that the flames are much closer to the grates, and your grill marks will be more defined. Whatever you do, make sure that when you lay something on a grill rack, you leave it sit for a few minutes to start to cook. If you try to turn it right away, it will stick.

I don't recommend grill pans or indoor electric grills because they lack the authentic grill flavor. If you must use them, they will work, but keep in mind that some flavor will be sacrificed because of the absence of the flames.

Roasting

Roasting is a fantastic way to bring out the deep flavors from within your foods. This is a great indoor, rustic way of cooking. When roasting vegetables, you'll need a little oil on them first or they will shrivel up and dry out. I like roasting most vegetables on high heat and charring the edges so they stay juicy inside. When roasting vegetables, such as onions, garlic and, peppers, you can also cook them on low heat with some oil for a long period of time to bring out all their natural sugars. They will come out soft and sweet—good enough to eat on their own. The broiler in your oven is a wonderful way to get last-minute color on something before you serve it.

Sautéing

Sautéing is a classic—mushrooms in wine sauce, greens in garlic and oil, pan-seared tofu. Like an old black-and-white movie, this is what has been done so well for so long. Sautéing is not just letting something cook in a fry pan. It is an art! Don't think this is a saucepot or stew; sautéing relies as much on timing as grilling does. You have to stay with your pan from start to finish, making sure the oil is at the right temperature and that you don't burn or overcook your food. To know how to sauté is to be a good cook. We will show you when to add your wine, how to keep your garlic from burning, and how to make sure your sauce is just right in the end.

Measuring

One pet peeve I have about cookbooks is the fact that they rely on measuring to the point where the techniques and knowledge of ingredients and their properties are lost underneath the tablespoons and behind the cups. I decided that if I was going to do a cookbook, I was going to try to teach people how to cook. This is art—not science. I think that it's important to come away from each recipe with knowledge of the technique that you just completed. You can always say "Yeah, I did it," but what is most important is being able to say, "I learned how to do it."

Salting Tomatoes

One of our favorite restaurant tricks is salting tomatoes. Cut some nice red-ripe tomatoes into approximately ½ - to 1-inch dice and place them in a mixing bowl. Then, sprinkle a nice shot of sea salt on them, toss them, and put them in the fridge for about 20 to 30 minutes. If your tomatoes were good, your knife sharp, and your dice small enough, the salt will have released the tomatoes' water and you will have at the bottom of your bowl some liquid gold.

I like to use tomato water in raw dishes a lot. It's the perfect liaison between your citrus and olive oil, providing that all-important middle ground between your fat and acid. In that same concept, it's a great addition to salad dressings.

Tomato water is also a great way to finish a from-scratch pasta sauce. Once you have cooked your tomatoes to your liking and are ready to toss your pasta in, pour in some tomato water with some extra virgin olive oil. This adds a last high note of fresh-garden flavor to a cooked sauce.

Blending versus Food Processing

In many of our recipes, we will call specifically for a food processor or specifically for a blender. The two machines are essential kitchen machines, but are not inter-changeable.

For instance, if you make a pesto in the food processor like you should, it will come out coarse and chunky with a multi-hued green texture. It will dance through your angel hair pasta in little flecks and tiny chunks. Put the same ingredients in a blender, and you will end up with a watery, bitter, green smoothie that is completely pulverized.

The same goes in the opposite. If you want to make a mango cream sauce with vegan sour cream and fresh mango, a blender will give it a silky smooth puree. The same ingredients in a food processor will look like a curdled chunky mess.

Roughly Chopping

You'll see the expression "roughly chopped" used throughout this book. This simply refers to a food item that will eventually be pureed or blended. You will want the vegetables cut into manageable chunks so that they cook through and blend easily, but you don't want to waste time by making the cuts and sizes perfect.

Common Ingredients for Savory Foods

Citrus

Lemon and lime juice are amazing high notes to add to a dish. What could be better than a black bean and avocado taco with a fresh squeeze of lime, or maybe a flame-grilled portobella with rosemary and a shot of fresh lemon? They are precious notes indeed in your culinary symphony. So don't play out of tune.

You know what I'm talking about, that bottle of ancient lemon juice with the plastic cap from the juice aisle of the supermarket or that syrupy lime goo behind your bar. Please throw them out right now. They are not citrus, they are crimes against citrus, and you may not use them for anything in this book.

Cut fresh lemon, cut fresh lime. Squeeze some juice for lemonade or limeade or for use in your cocktails. Have wedges on hand for dishes that need that last burst of brightness. Use what you need, and throw the rest out within 48 hours. Citrus loses its vitamin C very rapidly after being cut, which means it's deteriorating. If ever in doubt, use a fresh one.

Herbs

Here are a few words about herbs. Fresh herbs are so accessible these days. They are inexpensive and add a world of fresh flavor to whatever you are cooking. Don't be afraid to buy that pack of rosemary if you only need a couple of sprigs. Whatever you don't use of your fresh herbs just put them in a empty wine or olive oil bottle and fill it with olive oil, now you have a beautiful herb-infused oil to serve with bread at the table. Just remember to keep the herbs completely covered in oil so that they don't oxidize and go bad. I am not a huge fan of dried herbs, although I do use some in sauce and soup bases. Always follow the golden rule: dried herbs to start, fresh herbs to finish.

To get the perfect end result, follow the cookbook's guidelines about which herbs to use when and **don't ever substitute fresh for dried or vice versa**. It just doesn't work! Here's a brief rundown of some common herbs, and how the dried version works compared to fresh.

- **Basil** – This is the world's most incredible fresh herb. Need I say more? By contrast, it is just about the worst dried herb I can imagine.

- **Chives** – Ever since having fresh chives suspended in a Provençale Mustard Vinaigrette, I have been crazy for them. When chopped, they add striking visual appearance. Left whole, they are a dramatic garnish. The light spring-onion flavor is never too invasive, and dried chives actually work in a soup base if needed.

- **Cilantro** – Cilantro is a very popular herb nowadays with a great fresh flavor. It wakes up any Latin dish and makes a great fresh simple salsa with just onions and tomatoes. But again, this one just doesn't dry well at all.

- **Dill** – I love fresh dill used sparingly, and it goes great with lemon, red onion, and capers on smoked tofu or with grilled mushrooms. Dried dill is actually an interesting flavor, though it bears little resemblance to its fresh counterpart.

- **Oregano** – Oregano is the pizza herb! Most people are more familiar with the dry version than the fresh one. I love dried oregano on my pizza and in my spaghetti sauce, but fresh oregano will capture your heart when you try it. It is a classic, romantic flavor that transports you to the Italian Riviera.

- **Parsley** – I love both flat- and curly-leaf fresh parsley, which provides a brilliant fresh flavor that finishes any dish with a bright garden note. Its dried version is terrible.

- **Rosemary and Sage** – These two powerful fresh flavors should be finely chopped and used sparingly. They add the haunting backdrop for dishes on those first chilly nights of autumn, when you break out that bottle of red wine you have been saving. They both dry fairly well and make a nice foundation for dark winter sauces.

- **Tarragon and Chervil** – These classic and irreplaceable French herbs provide pleasing anise notes and fresh green flavor. In dried form, they just don't work.

- **Thyme** – Thyme goes with almost any cuisine. Sautéed thyme and onions is one of my favorite food aromas. Splash in some white wine to deglaze, and you're in heaven. Thyme dries pretty well and makes a great foundation flavor for a wide variety of French and Italian sauces.

Mayo, Vegan Mayo

There are several types of vegan mayonnaise on the market these days, but I love Vegenaise® with the blue label. Recipes that call for mayo in this cookbook have been built around this brand. Like a traditional mayonnaise, it is heavy, so use it in moderation.

Mustard

Mustard is an amazing dimension of flavor. I swear by Dijon mustard in my cooking and suggest that you buy only a quality Dijon for these recipes, such as Grey Poupon®. The cheap Dijon mustards bear almost no resemblance to the quality brands. I also like to keep on hand a grainy coarse mustard for more rustic dishes. Mustard doesn't go bad, so spend a little extra on this precious ingredient.

Oil

A good oil is essential for good cooking. However, like knives, you really don't need a lot of different kinds to prepare a great meal. I prefer to have two main oils on hand, a neutral oil for cooking and a really nice extra virgin olive oil for finishing. Olive oil comes in several grades: extra virgin, virgin, pomace, and pure.

Extra virgin olive oil—perhaps one of the world's greatest foods is not great to cook with, but is best used to finish dishes and for salads. You can keep it in the fridge, but it may coagulate. If it does, just bring it to room temperature for about 20 minutes before using it. Drizzle extra virgin olive oil on your hot pasta, grilled tofu, roasted vegetables, and antipasto just before serving. Its fruity, rich flavor is Mediterranean heaven. My golden rule, again, is to spend a few bucks for quality and buy small quantities often.

Pomace, pure, and light olive oils bear little resemblance to extra virgin in flavor, but are pretty good for cooking. Other neutral oils that are also good for cooking are soybean, canola, and safflower. These all stand up pretty well to high-heat cooking.

Two other oils that I like to keep in my pantry are toasted sesame oil, which is essential for Asian dishes, and white truffle oil, which is essential for everything else.

Salt

Very simply put, salt is the best way to enhance existing flavors. We never use salt to make a dish "salty," rather we use just enough to make the flavors shine. At the restaurant, we swear by sea salt and keep both the coarse and fine around for different uses.

Soy Sauce, Tamari

Soy sauce is a generalization, and when you buy an inexpensive product, which is simply labeled "soy sauce," you are doing your cooking a huge injustice. Tamari is a fermented soybean liquid that is full of exotic, mysterious flavor. Buy quality soy sauce, just like you would a good red wine or single malt scotch. Tamari is the Japanese version, which is my choice, although shoyou, which is the Chinese version, is perfectly acceptable. Yes, they are salty, but when you buy a quality tamari or shoyou and use it properly, you get a rich, dark depth of flavor.

Spices

Spices are the aromatic-wonder ingredients that make a flavor foundation in your cooking. Don't keep spices too long; their potency will fade. Buy them in small containers, and buy them often. Use dashes here and there to add interesting dimension to your sauces and soups. Spices should be very subtle on the palate. For instance, I love cumin, but I don't want to really taste it in my final dish. It should support and enhance the other ingredients, not dominate them. Like dry herbs, spices need to cook to dissipate their flavor.

I especially love Latin spices, like achiote, paprika, cumin, coriander, and allspice. I also love curry powder blends. I think I've tried almost every brand on the market and some that aren't.

Throughout this book you will see "Latin Spice blend" or "Island Spice blend." We custom blend our spices at the restaurant, and the following recipes are very similar to what we use. If you don't want to go to the trouble of mixing them, by all means, buy a pre-blended mix from the market. Just make sure that salt isn't the first ingredient, which is usually the sign of a lower-quality mix. You can use these market mixes, but make sure that you adjust you salt accordingly throughout the rest of the recipe.

Latin Spice

2 tablespoons paprika
1 tablespoon cumin
1 tablespoon granulated onion
1 tablespoon granulated garlic
1 tablespoon salt
1 tablespoon black pepper
2 teaspoons thyme
2 teaspoons oregano
1 tablespoon ground dry chile of your
   choice, such as chipotle, ancho or
   cayenne

Island Spice

1 tablespoon paprika
1 tablespoon cumin
1 tablespoon granulated onion
1 tablespoon granulated garlic
1 tablespoon salt
1 tablespoon black pepper
1 teaspoon nutmeg
¼ teaspoon clove
1 teaspoon ground ginger
2 teaspoons allspice
2 teaspoons thyme
2 teaspoons brown sugar

Here are some other indispensable Horizon spices:

- **Achiote** – From annatto seeds, this haunting spice is found all over the tropics. Its terra-cotta-brick-like color and earthy aromas take beans and vegetable stews to an exotic new level.

- **Allspice** – Almost all of the world's allspice is grown in Jamaica, and its actually sometimes called "Jamaica pepper." This dried berry will probably remind you more of a Christmas, pumpkin pie, or apple cider spice, but its origins are tropical. It has a wonderful sweet-spicy aroma. Try adding it to a curry for that island touch. Allspice is also a necessity in jerk sauce, but use it sparingly. It can get overly pungent very quickly.

- **Cumin** – Cumin is earthy, nutty, and complex. Overdo it once, and you will hate it forever. Subtly layer it into your bean dishes, letting the cumin flavor mingle with your onions, garlic, and tomatoes . For the best result, buy quality whole cumin seeds (not at a convenience store), toast them in a pan over low heat until you just start to smell them, and then grind them in a coffee mill. Wow!

- **Fennel Seed** – Use this powerful, licorice-anise flavor in your tomato sauce when you start cooking (put them in whole or slightly crushed). It's a great tomato-friendly accent.

- **Nutmeg** – As with allspice, nutmeg is another holiday spice with tropical origins. Almost all of the world's nutmeg comes from Grenada. In fact, in many places on the island, you can actually smell it in the air. Visit this beautiful island, have a rum punch with fresh nutmeg grated on top, and you will have a new tropical friend in your spice repertoire. Nutmeg and mace (the outer layer of the nutmeg) are very pungent and can be overdone quite easily. Use it with restraint.

- **Paprika (Smoked)** – This is one of my favorite secret weapons in the kitchen. It provides powerful, smoky flavors without the heat of chipotle. It's great on french fries or papas bravas (Spanish fried potatoes).

- **Seafood Seasoning** – An aromatic blend of spices that usually include bay leaf and celery seed. Never buy a cheap seafood seasoning. Although there are some good ones out there, the best by far is Old Bay®.

- **Saffron** – Saffron is the embodiment of the French and Spanish Riviera. This amazingly aromatic miracle flavor is expensive indeed, but there is no substitute. Luckily, a little goes a long way.

- **White pepper** – The French love to use this spice in cream sauces so that there are no black flecks, but to me, this spice is 100-percent Asian across the board. Add white pepper to miso soup, fried rice, lo mein noodles, edamame, etc .

Vegetable Stock

A good vegetable stock is an absolute key component in good cooking. Remember the stockpot is not a garbage pail; onion skins and carrot tops belong in your compost heap! What follows is a suggested recipe for making vegetable stock from scratch. However, for recipes in this book, I highly recommend finding a cube, powder, or liquid stock that you like. Choose one that you would eat on its own, then you know you have a great product that won't need adjusting down the line.

Ingredients

6 quarts water
1 pound carrots, ends trimmed and roughly chopped
5 stalks celery, with leaves and roughly chopped
1 large bunch leeks , washed thoroughly and roughly chopped
2 cloves garlic
2 teaspoons salt
2 teaspoons pepper
1 bunch asparagus bottoms (the bottom third of the stalks)
5 bay leaves
2 tablespoons canola oil

Directions

1. In a very large stockpot, heat the canola oil until almost smoking, and all the vegetables, except the asparagus.
2. Let cook in the oil for 3 to 5 minutes, but don't let the vegetables scorch.
3. Add the water and turn the heat to low and simmer for 25 minutes.
4. After 25 minutes, add the asparagus bottoms and simmer 5 more minutes.
5. Strain the stock into another pot or bucket through a strainer or colander, and mash the vegetables with the back of a spoon to extract extra flavor.
6. Discard the vegetables.
7. Taste the stock, and depending on your vegetables, it may be good to go. If not, return to the heat and simmer, letting the stock reduce by a fourth to concentrate the flavors and adjust salt to your taste.
8. Freeze what you will not use within 3 days.

Vinegar

In our cooking classes, I always stress the importance of vinegar, since it is the "fine wine" of cooking. Quality vinegars are complex and mysterious. They add the precious high note of acidity to rich dishes. They also add the zing to an olive-oil-based dressing or sauce. A little drop wakes up flat dishes that need that special something. So why in the world would you buy that giant plastic bottle for $1.99? It's garbage and should only be used it to clean your windows.

I have always thought that vinegar should be sold in small 1-ounce bottles for a very high price. Then people would use it with sparingly and with restraint—they way it should be used. Buy quality vinegar in small bottles and spend some money. It doesn't go bad, and will reward you in ways you never thought a vinegar could.

At the restaurant, we use a cherry-wood-aged balsamic that pours beautifully rich and a little thick. I also really like a good, aged sherry vinegar for marinated vegetables. For light sauces, use a nice French white wine vinegar or an Asian rice wine vinegar.

Wine

It's incredible how cooking with wine can take your dishes to new levels. Even if you don't drink alcohol, don't be afraid to cook with a little wine. It's not about the alcohol, which cooks off anyway in a matter of seconds. What you are left with is the essence of the fermented grape, and it does wonders and adds sophistication to your dish.

When cooking with wine, it is important to use a decent brand. You don't need the best wine in the world to cook, but we all know that we shouldn't cook with wine that we wouldn't drink. You can get a nice bottle of white wine, like Chardonnay or Sauvignon Blanc, for $7 or $8. You also can get a suitable bottle of red wine, like Cabernet Sauvignon or Merlot, for about $10. ▪

MIAMIGO

It's funny how Key West is called the "end of the road." In a sense, it is at mile marker 0, the end of Route A1A. Also ending in the keys is the intercoastal waterway, which technically begins in Maine, but is continuous from Maryland to the Keys. Florida itself is where the eastern United States ends. Down past the Appalachian and Smokey Mountains, through the rolling hills of Georgia, the land starts to flatten out just like going to the beach...one big beach before the endless ocean. How ironic it is that for our new immigrant influx, Florida is just the beginning.

Miami is what I like to call the new Ellis Island of the United States. The first site of the new world is no longer the Statue of Liberty, but Miami Beach and its high rises. It is now the age of Latin America, and in Miami, the immigrants are coming in full force. With them, they bring their food.

English is fast becoming a second language in Miami, but that's fine with me. In Miami, you can now authentically tour the culinary world of Latin America without a passport: Brazilian, Cuban, Argentine, Mexican, Nicaraguan, Peruvian, Venezuelan, Puerto Rican, Salvadorian, Bahamian and Caribbean. You can sample them all in a good day.

So as American Airlines flight 969 takes us back to snowy 29-degree Philadelphia this March evening, I look out along the eastern seaboard and try to drift back to my tropics. As we head north, the degrees in latitude increase while the degrees in Fahrenheit decrease. It's going to be cold. It's hard to believe that standing on the Jersey shore, you can turn your head to the right, look far down the sands, down to the south where the palms start to grow, down further yet to where the land flattens out, into the sprawling gateway to Latin America.

I will always have a deep passion for all the great cuisines of the world, but I am especially thankful for the Hispanic contribution and how it has helped shape my cooking at Horizons. The American melting pot now has a little spice in it, a squeeze of lime, and a fresh cilantro garnish. It's America's new stew. Bring your chips! ▪

SOUPS SOUPS

Ingredients

3 tablespoons canola or olive oil
1 red bell pepper, diced
1 large onion, diced
¼ cup garlic, chopped
10 plum tomatoes, roughly chopped
4 quarts vegetable stock
1 medium boniato (or sweet potato),
    peeled and diced
2 cups calabaza (or butternut squash),
    peeled, seeded, and diced
1 medium to large malanga (or
    potato), peeled and diced
3 carrots, peeled and diced
2 green plantains, peeled and diced
3 tablespoons Latin Spice blend
2 tablespoons tomato paste
3 tablespoons sugar

Yields

8 to 10 servings as an appetizer or
4 to 6 servings as an entrée

Ajiaco Criollo

This dish fascinates me—a Cuban stew of every imaginable root vegetable and different meats and fish. We'll leave the animals out of this, of course! The vegetables listed below are becoming increasingly available at supermarkets in many areas, but feel free to omit what you don't have and substitute with the ones I have suggested.

If, by any chance, you live in a little stone cottage on a deserted beach, may I suggest you simmer this stew in a big, black iron crock over an open fire near a palm tree and give us a call—we'll be right there.

Directions

1. In a large stockpot, with oil heated to high, add the onion, bell pepper, and garlic and brown for 3 to 4 minutes.

2. Add the tomatoes and Latin Spice blend and sauté 3 to 4 more minutes (this paste is called a *sofrito*).

3. Add the stock and all other ingredients and then simmer for 30 minutes on medium-low heat.

4. Garnish with lime wedges and/or plantain chips.

Brazilian Black Bean Soup

Pictures of Brazil haunt me. It is high on my list of places we must go. Someday, our footprints will be in the sands of the shores on the postcards of my dreams: Recife, Copacabana, and Impanema. Then there is the Amazon—the rainforest of all rainforests! Manaus is the city where the Amazon adventure begins. Until then, I have my postcards and my love of Brazilian cuisine—heavy on the chiles, coconut milk, and cilantro. What more can a lover of tropical food ask for?

Directions

1. In a large stockpot, bring all the ingredients, except the coconut milk, tomatoes, and cilantro to a simmer and cook for 10 minutes.

2. Carefully puree half the soup in a blender, or use an immersion blender to puree it to a creamy liquid, and return to the soup pot, or you can leave it brothy if you prefer.

3. Add the coconut milk and tomatoes, and simmer for an additional 2 to 3 minutes.

4. Remove from heat and add the cilantro on top.

5. Garnish with fresh lime wedges.

Ingredients

2 quarts vegetable stock (a little less if you like thick black bean soup, and a little less if you have reserved cooking liquid from cooking the beans yourself)
6 cups black beans, either from a can (drained and rinsed) or from scratch in a pressure cooker (in that case save some of the cooking liquid)
1 medium onion, diced
2 cloves garlic, chopped
1 green chile, chopped (anaheim, jalapeno, or habanero, if you dare, and leave the seeds in for even extra heat!)
2 tablespoons Latin Spice blend
1 cup coconut milk
1 cup tomatoes, diced
½ cup fresh cilantro, chopped

Yields

6 to 10 servings as an appetizer or 4 to 6 servings as an entrée

Calabaza Puree with Roasted Cinnamon Oil

Calabaza Puree with Roasted Cinnamon Oil

If you haven't tried calabaza yet, then now is the time! Calabaza is a Caribbean pumpkin with a texture and taste resembling butternut squash. Calabaza is plentiful in the Caribbean islands as well as Central and South America, and it is becoming increasingly available in northern climates. Make sure to save the seeds and roast them like you would pumpkin seeds—a great snack or an additional garnish for the soup. Substitute butternut squash if you like.

Directions for the Oil

1. Roast cinnamon at 500 degrees for 15 minutes.

2. Steep the hot cinnamon sticks in the ½ cup of canola oil for at least 45 minutes.

3. Add dashes of salt and sugar as desired for a more pronounced flavor.

Directions for the Soup

1. In a large pot, bring all ingredients, except the coconut milk, to a simmer and cook for 15 minutes.

2. Add the coconut milk and remove from heat; let rest for at least 5 minutes.

3. In small batches, carefully puree in a blender, or use an immersion blender to puree to a creamy liquid.

4. Pour soup into cups and drizzle (or "float") cinnamon oil on top.

Ingredients for the Oil

3 cinnamon sticks rubbed with canola oil
½ cup canola oil

Ingredients for the Soup

2 quarts vegetable stock
6 cups calabaza, roughly chopped with skin and seeds removed
1 cup onion, chopped
3 garlic cloves
2 tablespoons ginger, peeled and chopped
2 tablespoons Latin Spice blend
2 teaspoons sugar
4 carrots, peeled and chopped
2 potatoes, peeled and chopped
1 teaspoon salt
1 teaspoon pepper
2 cups coconut milk

Yields

6 to 10 servings as an appetizer or 4 to 6 servings as an entrée

Ingredients

2 quarts vegetable stock
1 (16-ounce) can tomatoes, crushed
   or pureed
10 plum tomatoes, roughly chopped
½ medium onion, chopped
4 cloves garlic, peeled and chopped
2 tablespoons ginger, peeled and
   chopped
2 tablespoons Island Spice blend
1 (16-ounce) can pinto or kidney
   beans, drained and rinsed
3 tablespoons sugar
1 very ripe plantain or banana (skin
   almost black)
1 teaspoon blackstrap molasses
½ cup dark rum
 3 cups coconut milk
Dash of allspice (optional)
Collard greens, finely chopped
   (optional)

Yields

6 to 10 servings as an appetizer

Jamaican Tomato & Red Bean Bisque

It was at Alfred's on the beach in Negril, Jamaica, that I had a wonderful meal of red beans and rice, accompanied by a crepe stuffed with callaloo, a Caribbean green that is similar to collards. The crepe was topped with a homemade Jamaican hot chile sauce. It was the perfect local food snack, my reward for leaving the hotel confines to seek out the authentic experience beyond the tourist perimeter.

Jamaican cuisine is one of the greatest of all in the Caribbean, full of exotic spice and deep flavor. It also happens to be very vegetarian friendly.

You'll love the thick, but smooth texture of this soup with its sweet hint of plantain on a layer of rum and coconut milk.

Directions

1. In a large pot, combine all ingredients, except the rum and coconut milk, and simmer for 15 to 20 minutes.

2. Add the rum and coconut milk and simmer for an additional 3 minutes.

3. In small batches, carefully puree in a blender, or use an immersion blender to puree to a creamy liquid.

4. Garnish with a dash of ground allspice or finely chopped collards.

Note: You can add a touch more sugar if your plantains or tomatoes are not sweet enough.

Japanese Noodle Bowl with Edamame

This is a great 'meal soup' to have as a lunch on a cold day. Not only will it warm you from the inside out, it is also physically nourishing. I love soba noodles, but use what you like. Even leftover spaghetti will work just fine.

I recommend a white miso here because it is very mild. Miso also comes in darker varieties, such as red or barley. If you are a fan of miso, then by all means, use a darker miso—it will add that much more flavor intensity to the soup. One golden rule of miso: never boil it, since boiling kills all of its nutritional value.

Directions

1. In a large pot, bring the stock, garlic, ginger, white pepper, sugar, and onion to a simmer. Simmer 5 minutes.

2. Add the bok choy, snow peas, noodles, and edamame and continue to simmer for another 2 minutes.

3. Remove from heat and stir in the tamari, sesame oil, and miso.

4. Portion into bowls, using tongs to lift out the noodles.

5. Garnish with the nori, scallions, and sesame seeds. Add some wasabi powder if you like.

Ingredients

2 quarts vegetable stock
2 tablespoons garlic, chopped
3 tablespoons ginger, grated or minced
1 teaspoon white pepper
2 teaspoons sugar
1 medium onion, slivered
1 large head of bok choy, cleaned and chopped
2 cups snow peas or snap peas
1 (16-ounce) package of soba, udon, or other noodle of your choice (cooked and chilled)
1 (12-ounce) bag frozen shelled edamame beans, thawed
¼ cup tamari soy sauce
3 tablespoons toasted sesame oil
½ cup white miso paste
1 sheet nori seaweed, cut into thin strips with scissors
2 scallions, chopped
Sesame seeds
Wasabi powder (optional)

Yields

6 to 10 servings as an appetizer or
4 to 6 servings as an entrée

Ingredients

2 quarts vegetable stock
4 cups seitan, chopped
1 cup onion, diced
1 cup dark ale
4 cloves garlic, crushed
2 teaspoons dried thyme
2 teaspoons dried sage
1 teaspoon salt
1 teaspoon black pepper
2 teaspoons sugar
2 tablespoons margarine
1 cup dried wild mushroom blend
2 cups pre-cooked barley, prepared
   according to package
Chives, chopped (optional)
Drizzle truffle oil (optional)
Baguette slices (optional)

Yields

6 to 10 servings as an appetizer or
4 to 6 servings as an entrée

Seitan Beef, Barley & Ale Soup

As much as I love the tropics, by contrast, I am absolutely obsessed with England. I just love the place and always have ever since I was little. My favorite worlds meet in the English Caribbean on islands like Bermuda and Barbados, but my favorite discovery was a little place called Green Turtle Cay in the Northern Bahamas. After a short boat ride from Treasure Cay in the Abacos, I arrived in New Plymouth on Green Turtle Cay—one of the coolest, little islands I have ever seen. A 15-minute golf cart ride through a dirt road in the pine forest leads to a little slice of England. The Green Turtle Cay Club was complete with a fireplace, Queen Anne chairs, and afternoon tea! Very cool. No tropical adventure is complete without a little tribute to mother England.

Directions

1. In a large pot, simmer all ingredients, except the barley, for 15 minutes.

2. Stir in the barley and simmer for an additional 5 minutes.

3. Garnish with fresh, chopped chives, truffle oil, or toasted baguette slices.

Seitan Gumbo

You don't see that much Cajun/Creole food around here these days. Perhaps it was a passing culinary fad. In New Orleans, it is still a way of life, except for the animals, of course!

I have always loved Cajun/Creole food. The deep, deep flavors, the spices, and the French accents make it irresistible. This recipe is a bit more involved than the others, but the results are well worth it.

File (pronounced fee-lay) powder is obtained from the inside of a pod from the sassafras tree. It helps thicken the gumbo, but I like to let the roux (pronounced rue) do that. For me, file powder adds an unmistakable and irreplaceable flavor to the gumbo. Try it!

Ingredients

2 quarts vegetable stock
4 cups seitan, chopped
1 large onion, diced
3 celery stalks, diced
2 green bell peppers, diced
2 cups okra, diced
6 plum tomatoes, diced
2 tablespoons Latin Spice blend
1 (16-ounce) can red pinto or kidney
    beans, drained and rinsed
2 tablespoons ketchup
1 teaspoon sugar
2 teaspoons gumbo file powder
3 tablespoons flour
3 tablespoons margarine

Yields

6 to 10 servings as an appetizer or
4 to 6 servings as an entrée

Directions

1. In a large pot, combine all ingredients except the file powder, flour, and margarine.

2. Bring to a simmer and remove from heat after 15 minutes.

3. Meanwhile, in a saucepan, start the roux by combining the flour and margarine or oil. Stir with a wooden spoon over medium-low heat until you get a nice golden brown paste (about 8 to 10 minutes).

   Note: For a deeper, richer flavor, you can continue to brown the roux until it looks like peanut butter. Keep in mind that the darker the roux, the less thickening power it will have.

4. Return the soup to a simmer and gently, but thoroughly, whisk in the roux a little at a time.

5. Add the file powder.

6. When the soup comes to a boil, cook it for 1 minute longer only, which will ensure that the roux has properly and fully thickened.

Ingredients

2 quarts vegetable stock
15 plum tomatoes, roughly chopped
1 large onion, roughly chopped
6 cloves garlic, minced
4 pinches saffron threads
1 dash cumin
2 tablespoons sugar
2 teaspoons salt
2 teaspoons pepper
1 medium leek, washed and cut into
   thin rings
2 (12-ounce) jars artichokes, chopped
1 (16-ounce) bag frozen peas, thawed
1 red bell pepper, very finely chopped
½ cup sherry wine
2 tablespoons extra virgin olive oil
1 cup precooked rice

Yields

6 to 10 servings as an appetizer or
4 to 6 servings as an entrée

Spanish Tomato-Artichoke Soup with Peas

I have a deep affection for Spanish cuisine. After all, it was the Spaniards who brought their tomatoes, peppers, and spices to the Americas (albeit by conquest) to mingle with the indigenous staples that helped give us what is today Latin American food. But classic Spanish food is so intriguing on its own. The simmering of saffron, tomatoes, garlic, and wine is an enchanting combination of aromas sure to captivate your senses.

We celebrated our second wedding anniversary in Barcelona and on the stunning island of Mallorca. We went from tapas bar to tapas bar, an unforgettable food experience! This soup embodies some of the incredible flavors that I will forever love about Spain.

Directions

1. In a large pot, combine all ingredients except the leeks, artichokes, peas, red pepper, sherry, extra virgin olive oil, and rice, and simmer for 20 minutes on medium heat.

2. Let cool slightly and then puree with an immersion blender or regular blender.

3. Return the puree to the heat, add the remaining ingredients, and simmer for an additional 5 to 7 minutes.

4. Garnish with a fresh splash of sherry and the extra virgin olive oil.

Spanish Tomato-Artichoke Soup with Peas

Thai Tofu & Cabbage Soup with Curry Roasted Peanuts

Thai Tofu & Cabbage Soup with Curry Roasted Peanuts

What more can you ask for than coconut, peanuts, and curry? Thai food is a palate pleaser, and this easy soup will make an exotic impression as a first course.

Thai curry pastes are one of my favorite food products. These pastes pack so much flavor. Make sure to read the ingredients—some contain shrimp or fish paste. The yellow and green are great, but the red will work best in this soup.

Use this soup base to explore combinations other than the tofu/nappa one that I have outlined. Try cauliflower or broccoli, or a blend of Asian vegetables like baby corn, bamboo shoots, and water chestnuts. I'm often inspired to make this soup when I return from the local Asian market with boxes full of hard-to-find Asian greens like Shanghai tips, Yu-Choy, or Taiwanese bok choy.

Ingredients for the Peanuts

1 cup raw peanuts
½ teaspoon salt
2 teaspoons curry powder
2 tablespoons canola oil

Ingredients for the Soup

2 quarts vegetable stock
16 ounces tofu, cut into 1-inch cubes
1 teaspoon canola oil
1 head nappa cabbage, finely chopped
1 medium onion, thinly sliced
4 cloves garlic, crushed
3 tablespoons ginger, peeled and finely chopped or grated
¼ cup creamy peanut butter
2 cups coconut milk
2 tablespoons sugar
2 teaspoons red, yellow, or green curry paste
1½ teaspoons salt
Red chile paste (optional)
Scallions, chopped (optional)

Yields

6 to 10 servings as an appetizer

Directions for the Peanuts

1. Toss the peanuts with the salt, curry powder, and oil.

2. Place coated peanuts on a baking tray and bake for 8 minutes at 400 degrees.

3. Allow to cool, then crush the peanuts in a food processor or with a knife.

Directions for the Soup

1. Roast the tofu or sauté it in a wok on high heat with 1 teaspoon canola oil for the most flavor.

2. Then, combine all ingredients in a large pot and bring to a simmer for 10 minutes.

3. Serve the soup with the peanuts on top, and add chopped scallion for garnish if you like.

Ingredients

8 cucumbers, peeled and seeded
½ cup onion, chopped
1 bunch fresh cilantro, leaves only
½ cup fresh mint leaves (packed)
4 tablespoons fresh lime juice
1 clove garlic
2 tablespoons olive oil
2 teaspoons salt
2 teaspoons pepper
1 teaspoon sugar
¼ cup vegan mayo

Yields

4 to 8 servings as an appetizer

Summer Cucumber Soup
with Cilantro & Mint

This nice, light, chilled soup is a perfect barefoot lunch starter. To create a raw version, use agave syrup as the sweetener and substitute one ripe avocado for the vegan mayo.

Directions

1. Puree all ingredients in a food processor, adding enough water to reach your desired consistency.

    Note: The soup should be fairly thick, but adjust to your liking.

2. Let chill for at least one hour before serving.

Vegan Key West Conch Chowder

Kate and I visited Key West a few years ago. After soaking in the Mallory Dock Sunset, we drifted over to Pepe's Bar where the crowd was jumping to live salsa music. We ordered mojitos and joined the crowd in a scene that I will never forget.

The band was incredible, and in the middle of a great jam, a Cuban couple in at least their 70s, but probably older, took the dance area by storm. In front of the band, this couple absolutely amazed us. They moved like they were kids, never missing a beat of the rhythm. Witnessing the passion of a music and food culture like Cuba's was so incredibly inspiring.

Billboards and souvenir shops aside, I love the keys and have always felt a connection there. This classic recipe is a vegetarian's passport to paradise.

Directions

1. Simmer all ingredients together for 15 minutes.

2. Garnish with plantain or boniato chips.

Ingredients

2 quarts vegetable stock
1½ cups textured vegetable protein (TSP) granules
2 cups tomato puree
1 cup bell pepper, diced
1 cup celery, diced
1 cup onion, diced
2 cups fresh or canned diced tomato
2 tablespoons habanero or jalapeno pepper, chopped (optional)
2 tablespoons Island Spice blend
2 tablespoons margarine
2 teaspoons seafood seasoning
2 cups raw potatoes, diced
2 teaspoons sugar
½ cup coconut milk
¼ cup dark rum
Plantain or boniato chips (optional)

Yields

6 to 10 servings as an appetizer or
4 to 6 servings as an entrée

Trio of Gazpachos

Direct from the Summer 2004 menu, this colorful, fresh, and healthy trio of chilled, raw soups was a huge hit. The three colors also come with three themes: red is the Spanish classic, yellow is the bright Caribbean version, and green, of course, is Mexican. Nothing is cooked, so you only need a trusty knife and a simple food processor. The end result is remarkable.

Red Ingredients

6 plum tomatoes
½ cup red bell pepper, seeded and white membrane removed
1 clove garlic
2 tablespoons extra virgin olive oil
½ teaspoon balsamic or sherry vinegar
5-6 fresh basil leaves
½ cup red onion, chopped
1 teaspoon salt
1 teaspoon pepper

Yellow Ingredients

3-4 large yellow tomatoes
¼ cup onion, chopped
1 teaspoon fresh ginger, peeled
½ teaspoon curry powder
1 dash ground allspice
1 tablespoon fresh lime juice
2 tablespoons canola oil
1 teaspoon brown sugar to taste
½ teaspoon salt to taste
½ teaspoon pepper

Green Ingredients

6 tomatillos, outer husks peeled
2 green bell or poblano peppers, seeded and white membrane removed
2 cucumbers, peeled and seeded
1 cup fresh cilantro leaves
2 tablespoons fresh lime juice
3 tablespoons canola oil
1 dash cumin
2 teaspoons agave syrup or sugar
One ripe avocado, peeled
2 teaspoons salt
1 teaspoon pepper

Directions

1. Puree ingredients for each soup (separately) in a food processor.
2. Mix ingredients for each soup and allow to sit at least 2 hours, preferably overnight.
3. Once thoroughly chilled, adjust salt to taste.

Trio of Gazpachos

Ingredients

2 quarts vegetable stock
2 heads cauliflower, leaves and center
    stem removed, broken into florets
2 (16-ounce) cans white beans
    (cannellini, great northern, or
    navy), drained and rinsed
1 cup onion, roughly chopped
4 cloves garlic
2 medium potatoes, peeled and
    chopped
2 teaspoons salt
1 teaspoon pepper
1 teaspoon dried sage
1 cup white wine
2 tablespoons olive oil
2 sprigs fresh rosemary
White truffle oil for garnish
Fresh herbs for garnish (chives or
    parsley, chopped)

Yields

6 to 10 servings as an appetizer or
4 to 6 servings as an entrée

White Bean & Cauliflower Puree with Truffle Oil

This luxuriously creamy soup is perfect for winter! If you have the time, I recommend cooking the white beans from scratch in a pressure cooker, or simmering them on a stovetop. One bag will equal the amount of canned beans called for below.

Truffle oil is amazing! One of my favorite things in the world. Don't buy a cheap one since there is a huge difference in quality. Always buy a quality truffle oil, and it will be your friend for life.

Now, light the fireplace and drift off to Northern Italy with a glass of red wine and some crusty bread…

Directions

1. In a large pot, bring all ingredients, except the rosemary, truffle oil, and garnishing herbs to a simmer for 15 minutes.

2. Drop in the rosemary and simmer for an additional 2 minutes.

3. Remove and discard the rosemary.

4. In small batches, carefully puree in a blender, or use an immersion blender to puree to a creamy liquid.

5. Portion soup into bowls and garnish with a generous drizzle of white truffle oil and fresh chopped herbs.

TRAVEL IS THE SPICE OF LIFE

In Early Childhood...

When I was a kid, my parents took my sisters and me to the west coast of Florida for a family vacation. Sanibel Island was one of my first visions of paradise. I remember the sand path from the hotel to the beach, surrounded by tropical foliage growing high up on either side. The path emptied out onto the beach, where this young jungle adventurer was rewarded with his first view of the glorious Gulf of Mexico.

Like most people who have been there, I remember Sanibel beach as being full of beautiful shells and driftwood and being very laid back. Since then, Sanibel has witnessed its share of development and hurricanes. I'm sure I would not recognize it now, but I hold on strong to those wonderful early visions of my paradise. It was enough to keep my heart in the tropics ever since.

Those early visions sparked my fascination with maps. It's our world after all. When the kids in my elementary school were busy learning the capitals of the United States, I daydreamed of mysterious areas at the far edges of the map. The islands of the Caribbean were, of course, my favorites. Strung out like a giant arch from Puerto Rico down to Venezuela are the bits and pieces of a floating lost world. Many of the islands are indeed the tips of submerged volcanoes, others a brief manifestation of land in an endless turquoise heaven of water.

Sharing some of that gorgeous water is Mexico, and it was here where I first developed a love affair with tropical foods. In fact, in all my travels there, I have always found good food. My parents first took us there when we were in our early teens. I was so entranced by the restaurant scenes. How cool a culture is it that starts a meal with chips and salsa instead of bread? One that boasts a national drink like the Margarita that goes with absolutely everything on the menu? Let's run down the list of reasons to worship this cuisine: cilantro, lime, chiles, rice, beans, tortillas, tomatoes, tomatillos, avocado, and tequila. That, my friends, I learned early on is a top-ten list to take to the beach!

As a Chef...

As I grew older and my love affair with travel continued, food took on even greater importance in choosing destinations. One year, my travels brought me to Grenada via an American Eagle island hopper from San Juan, Puerto Rico.

The San Juan International Airport is one of the most confusing places in the galaxy. While wandering through its mazes on the way to my connection, I caught sight of a giant sculpture map of the Caribbean posted on the wall in the main concourse. I was dazzled by it; my eyes traced the names of the islands just as I did when I was a kid with my school maps. My flight that day would pass over almost all of these islands on the way to the end of the Caribbean island chain.

What a flight it was! Through the windows on the left side of the plane, I passed every island I have grown to recognize only on paper. Now, one by one, these beautiful life-sized models floated before me. The beachless, giant cone, mountain world of Saba. Then Montserrat with its volcano still erupting, covered in clouds of volcanic ash and smoke. The Frenchies: Guadeloupe and Martinique. The untamed jungle world of lush Dominica, and the dramatic pitons of St. Lucia. Just like their pictures, just like the descriptions I had read over and over in travel books, I recognized them all at once, and I felt like I knew them.

Grenada is a fascinating place—friendly, lush, and beautiful. Its nickname, "the spice island," is so very fitting. I remember walking through the open-air markets in the main town of St. George. At a spice stand, I saw a sign that said "Saffron ... $1/lb." I couldn't believe my eyes! "I was Rich!!!" The world's most expensive spice for only $1 a pound???!!! Well, when I came to my senses, I realized that the sign was actually above a bin of some curious, knobby, ginger-like roots. It was actually fresh turmeric, which is what the islanders call saffron. If you happen to find fresh turmeric (try an

Indian market), pick some up for use in your curries and Caribbean dishes. Its beautiful color and delicate, distinct flavor add an exotic dimension to your dishes.

Grenada also grows much of the world's nutmeg. Again, if you haven't had fresh nutmeg, then you are missing out on something special. In Grenada, they grate it over rum punch for an unforgettably unique taste. Mace is the outer shell of the nutmeg. A bit different and more pungent than the actual nut, it's ground into a powder and used to spice up desserts and savory dishes.

My desire to eat local food has always been a challenge. The nicer hotels on islands such as Grenada usually serve a tutti-frutti interpretation of what tropical food is supposed to be. It's a cliché of papaya salsas and ginger beurre blancs prepared by a French-trained chef. It's fun and sometimes delicious, but it's not what the islanders eat. There are those times when you just have to throw caution to the wind, live dangerously, and hit the streets or the beach to find a little shack (the kind you would never set foot in back home) and order up some authentic, down-home grub.

My favorite tropical food story is not surprisingly about one of my favorite meals of all time. Antigua, ringed by some of the Caribbean's most incredible beaches, sets the stage for this culinary event. The island's Fig Tree Drive winds through a small rainforest of rolling hills, flowers, and banana palms set in a vibrant tapestry of lush, green textures.

On the way there, Kate and I drove past a curious-looking stand on the side of the road. There, under a thatch roof in the tropical midday sun, was a glorified food cart with a sign reading: "Ital Rasta Vegetarian." There were a few picnic benches and not a gringo in sight—our kind of place! On a table under the thatch roof were about 10 clay crocks with big lids. The vendor started explaining to me what each one contained as she lifted off the lids. With each lift rose a curling steam of aromatic herbs, spices, and coconut milk. It could have very easily been a dream.

In my gastronomic bliss, I just slurred out "please give me a little of everything." She loaded up our plates, spoonful by spoonful of these incredible, exotic stews, rice dishes, and vegetables, describing what they were as she went. We sat down in the shade and tasted one of the best plates of food we have ever eaten. The spices, the aromatics, the vegetables… all so brilliantly balanced and euphorically delicious. Perfect. I still dream of those flavors to this day.

Into the Future...

So what do the tropics mean to me today? They are a treasure chest of warm memories. I love to surf the waves of the net in January, looking at travel sites and reading tropical menus. When I find those bargain fares to Florida, we sneak down on Sunday morning, grab a car and head right for the beach. With our shoes kicked off, we literally just stand there and curl our toes in the sand, look north, and laugh at ourselves that just a few hours prior we were shivering in the cold of the harsh northeast winter. A few drinks and a few waterside meals later, we find ourselves back on the plane again, heading back home to the tundra, but armed with a little sunshine and warmth to keep us dreaming of the next ocean. ◼

SALADS

Dressing Ingredients

1 tablespoon white truffle oil
¼ cup vegan mayo
1 teaspoon Dijon mustard
½ teaspoon sherry vinegar
1 tablespoon fresh chives, chopped
Salt and pepper to taste
¼ cup olive oil

Salad Ingredients

2 to 3 tablespoons of a neutral oil,
   such as canola
1 large potato (Yukon gold works
   best), chopped into tiny dice about
   ½ inch or less
Salt and pepper to taste
2 to 3 heads of frisee lettuce (preferably baby), cleaned and left whole
1 medium very red tomato, cut into
   wedges for garnish

Yields

2 servings

Frisee Salad with Roasted Potatoes & Creamy Truffle Vinaigrette

This is one of my all-time favorite salads. It transports me instantly to the French countryside. Join us at a little café table in an herb garden with a bottle of white wine and a baguette for this perfect spring afternoon lunch.

Directions

1. Whisk together all dressing ingredients, except the olive oil.

2. Add the olive oil slowly, continuing to whisk until emulsified and set aside.

3. Heat the 2 or 3 tablespoons of oil in a sauté pan until it ripples and almost smokes.

4. Add the diced potatoes and sauté until they turn a deep golden brown.

5. Remove potatoes from the pan, drain on a paper towel, and sprinkle with a little salt and pepper. Set aside.

6. Dress the frisee, and add the potatoes on top while still warm.

7. Garnish with tomato wedges.

Frisee Salad with Roasted Potatoes & Creamy Truffle Vinaigrette

Dressing Ingredients

2 tablespoons fresh lemon juice
¼ cup vegan mayo
1 teaspoon Dijon mustard
¼ to ½ teaspoon each of salt and
    pepper, depending on taste

Salad Ingredients

1 (16-ounce) package of washed baby
    arugula
¼ cup oil-cured olives, pitted
½ cup red onion, sliced as thinly as
    possible

Yields

2 to 4 servings

Arugula Salad with Creamy Lemon Dressing, Oil-Cured Olives & Red Onion

Arugula is a magical salad green. Buy only the clean baby arugula, no bunched sandy stuff. For me, arugula's beauty comes from its intense, bitter nuttiness that actually ends up being another dimension of flavor in the dressing. This recommended dressing harmonizes so perfectly with arugula's qualities. Oil-cured olives are another of my favorite foods; their flavor is mysterious, deep, exotic, fruity, salty, and just plain addictive.

Directions

1. In a small mixing bowl, whisk all the dressing ingredients together and set aside.

   Note: Since arugula is a delicate green, the dressing should not be too thick. If it is too thick, then add a few drops of cold water to thin the dressing appropriately.

2. Slice the red onion as thinly as you can with a sharp knife and then add it to the salad bowl.

3. Roughly chop the olives and add them to the salad bowl.

4. Just prior to serving, toss the greens, olives, and onion with the dressing to make sure the greens stay fresh.

Caribbean Caesar Salad

Caesar salads have a notoriously heavy dressing. Here's a cleaned up Horizons vegan version. I think the spike of lime and island spice are touches that really make this dressing sparkle. For garnishes, try some yucca or plantain chips. The crunchiness adds a great dimension of texture and replaces the classic "crouton."

Directions

1. In a small mixing bowl, whisk all the dressing ingredients together and set aside.

2. Cut and wash the romaine lettuce. Dry it in a salad spinner or by patting it with paper towels. Set aside.

3. When you are ready to eat, toss the romaine with the dressing, making sure to coat all the lettuce evenly.

Dressing Ingredients

1½ tablespoon Dijon mustard
2 teaspoons Island Spice blend
1 teaspoon lime juice
¼ cup vegan mayo
2 tablespoons cold water
2 tablespoons canola, peanut, or
   sunflower oil
1 teaspoon sugar

Salad Ingredients

2 heads of romaine lettuce
   (use hearts if you prefer only the
   lighter, sweeter leaves)
Yucca or plantain chips (optional)

Yields

2 to 3 servings

Chopped Greek Salad

Chopped Greek Salad

Kate and I almost chose the Greek Islands for our honeymoon. When I see white stucco arches, I dream of Greece. I dream of this passionate food culture—beautiful plump olives, lemons, tomatoes, incredible peppers, and eggplant. Someday, hopefully in a small boat, we will journey deep into this fabled part of the Mediterranean—Rhodes, Mykonos, Crete, and the holy grail...Santorini!

I have recommended classic kalamata olives here, which are an icon of Greek cuisine, but this recipe will work with any olives. Feel free to use your favorites.

Directions

1. In a small mixing bowl, whisk all the dressing ingredients together and set aside.

2. Place all prepared salad ingredients together in a salad bowl and set aside.

3. When ready to eat, toss the salad ingredients with the dressing, making sure to coat it evenly.

4. If desired, serve with warmed pita bread, or toast the pita in the oven at 400 degrees for 20 minutes to make croutons.

Dressing Ingredients

3 tablespoons extra virgin olive oil
2 teaspoons red wine vinegar
1 teaspoon salt
1 teaspoon black pepper
¼ cup parsley, chopped
1½ tablespoons lemon juice

Salad Ingredients

1 cup kalamata olives, pitted and chopped
1 cup plum tomatoes, chopped
2 red bell peppers, roasted and sliced into strips
½ cup red onion, slivered
½ cup cucumber, chopped
½ cup smoked tofu, chopped
1 head romaine hearts, thinly sliced or shredded
Pita bread (optional)

Yields

2 servings

Dressing Ingredients

¼ cup fresh ginger, peeled
1 teaspoon garlic, crushed
1 cup carrots, peeled and chopped
¼ cup vegan mayo
1 teaspoon ketchup
1 teaspoon sesame oil
2 teaspoons sugar
1 teaspoon black pepper
1 teaspoon salt
1 teaspoon canola oil
½ cup cold water

Salad Ingredients

4 cucumbers, peeled and chopped
4 plum tomatoes, chopped into dice
2 scallions, chopped
2 cups fresh whole basil leaves

Yields

2 to 4 servings

Cucumber Salad with Hawaiian Ginger Dressing

I find it ironic that one of the easiest places to eat vegetarian is also where the food is so misunderstood. We're talking Hawaiian cuisine, too often manifested in a cliché of ham and pineapple pizza or mac nut coffee. I guess it's understandable when you realize that icons of Hawaiian culture include grass skirts, tiki dolls, leis, mai tais, and the hula.

Hawaiian cuisine, like its culture, runs so much deeper than the tackiness. It starts with the land itself. Hawaii is a land of truly breathtaking scenery. No words and no exaggeration can do it justice. From the spectacular Io Valley in Maui, to the fairy-tale wonderland of Hanalei Bay in Kauai, to the otherworld moonscapes and jungle waterfalls on the Big Island. This floating fantasy in the middle of the Pacific is truly an experience.

The fertile, volcanic soil is a haven for growing beautiful produce. Mostly organic and unbelievably abundant, the salad greens are amazing. The fruits, especially the papaya, are sensational. Macadamia nuts are not a tourist gimmick; they define Hawaiian cuisine and turn up everywhere, as does ginger, guava, and lilikoi (passion fruit). We'll give ginger the spotllight here in this beautifully colorful and tangy island dressing.

Directions

1. Puree all dressing ingredients in a food processor until smooth and set aside.

2. Prepare and arrange the salad ingredients in a salad bowl and set aside.

3. When ready to eat, toss the salad ingredients with the dressing, making sure to coat it evenly.

Suggested Variation

Serve mixture with lettuces if you like more of a leaf salad.

Malaysian Cabbage Salad with Peanut-Orange Dressing

Ever since my first taste of salads at Thai and Malaysian restaurants, I have been hooked on the incredible flavors and textures: powerful citrus, nutty peanut, sweet and creamy coconut-based dressings; crunchy cabbage; and fresh green papaya. Throw on some chiles and kaffir lime, and let that mingle with the final addition of fresh mint or basil. This is a salad with some attitude!

Directions

1. Blend all dressing ingredients together in a food processor until smooth and set aside.

2. Remove rough outer leaves from cabbage and shred with a food processor slicing blade or carefully by hand with a knife.

3. Arrange all salad ingredients in a salad bowl and set aside.

4. When ready to eat, toss the salad ingredients with the dressing, making sure to coat it evenly.

Dressing Ingredients

¼ cup fresh orange juice
2 tablespoons peanut butter
¼ cup peanut, sesame, or canola oil
½ cup coconut milk
1 teaspoon curry powder
1 tablespoon ground ginger from a jar or finely chopped peeled, fresh ginger
1 garlic clove
2 teaspoons sugar
2 tablespoons soy sauce
1 teaspoon red chile paste (Asian)

Salad Ingredients

½ head cabbage
2 scallions, sliced thinly on the bias
1 carrot, peeled and shredded

Yields

2 to 4 servings

Dressing Ingredients

¾ cup vegan mayo
¼ cup Dijon mustard
¼ cup olive oil
1 cup fresh cilantro leaves
¼ cup onion or shallot, chopped
1½ tablespoon fresh lime juice or
    2 tablespoons if you like your
    dressings tangy
¼ teaspoon salt
¼ teaspoon pepper
¼ cup water

Salad Ingredients

2 (12-ounce) bags baby spinach
    leaves, washed and trimmed
1 cup fresh tomatoes, diced
1 cup ripe avocado, diced
¼ cup jalapeno peppers, chopped
    (optional)
¼ cup red onion, sliced
Crushed tortilla chips to garnish

Yields

4 servings

Spinach Salad with Cilantro Dressing

Our Yucatan chopped spinach salad has been on our menu for as long as I can remember. At the restaurant, we chop everything finely, bind it in a creamy dressing, and pack it in a ring mold. When unmolded onto the plate, we garnish it with tortilla strips and have what Philadelphia Inquirer *restaurant critic Craig LaBan called " a spectacular tower...the most fiest-ive plate of roughage I've ever eaten."*

Here is a much simpler home version of that salad that you can enjoy without the tedious amounts of prep that go into the restaurant version.

Directions

1. Put all dressing ingredients in a food processor, puree until smooth, and place in the refrigerator until ready to use.

2. Place all salad ingredients, excluding the tortillas, in a large mixing bowl.

3. Add about half the dressing and toss thoroughly to coat.

    Note: Taste the salad to see if it's to your liking—some people like to really taste the spinach, while others like the richness of extra dressing. I think the perfect salad is when you can taste the greens and the dressing at the same exact time on your palate. Harmony is the key.

4. When you have the dressing adjusted to your liking, divide the mixture into four portions on plates.

5. Garnish with tortillas and serve immediately.

Spinach Salad with Cilantro Dressing

Tapas Salad with Pickled Garlic, Cumin & Lime Vinaigrette

Tapas Salad with Pickled Garlic, Cumin & Lime Vinaigrette

Spanish food is in style right now, and Kate and I really indulged on a recent end-of-summer trip to Barcelona and Mallorca. For me, Mallorca was love at first sight with its beautiful landscape, palm trees, incredible beaches, and the wonderful old and new town of Palma. However, it was the food that made this island so special. On mainland Barcelona, it only got better. We ate tapas and drank wine all day long while we toured the city, beaches, gothic quarter, and palm-lined boulevards. This is truly one of my favorite places in the world.

There are so many great imported Spanish tapas products in markets right now, so I designed this salad with its tangy, pickled garlic vinaigrette to highlight some interesting Spanish delicacies.

Directions

1. Blend all dressing ingredients together in a food processor until smooth and set aside.

2. Toss the greens with the blended vinaigrette.

3. Arrange the tapas on top of the dressed greens. If desired, add the optional almonds and fresh parsley as well.

4. Drizzle the entire arrangement with extra virgin olive oil and add some fresh cracked pepper.

Dressing Ingredients

¼ cup pickled garlic cloves (from a jar)
1 teaspoon ground cumin
2 tablespoons fresh lime juice
¼ cup olive oil
2 teaspoons Dijon mustard
1/8 cup water
Salt and pepper to taste

Salad Ingredients

Salad greens of your choice
   (**Note**: I find the whiter ones work best in this dish, such as romaine hearts or even iceberg.)
½ cup manzanilla or mantequilla olives, chopped
1 small jar white asparagus, drained
1 small jar unmarinated artichoke hearts, drained
1 small jar piquillo peppers, drained (substitute roasted red peppers if necessary)
2 tablespoons marcona almonds for garnish (optional)
2 tablespoons fresh parsley, chopped, for garnish (optional)
1 tablespoon extra virgin olive oil
Black cracked pepper to taste

Yields

2 servings

Dressing Ingredients

1 cup pistachios, shelled
1 tablespoon Dijon mustard
¼ teaspoon salt
¼ teaspoon pepper
½ teaspoon brown sugar
2 tablespoons sherry vinegar
1 cup olive oil
½ cup water
1 small garlic clove
1 tablespoon onion or shallot, roughly
   chopped

Suggested Salad Ingredients

Mix, match, expand, or just keep it
simple with red leaf lettuce and the
vinaigrette:

Baby red leaf lettuce (Lolla Rossa)
Baby red oak lettuce
Baby red romaine
Standard red leaf lettuce
Red onion, raw slices or roasted
   quarters
Roasted, grilled, or raw pears
Roasted golden beets
Roasted parsnips
Sliced grapes
Shredded red carrots
Shredded celery root (blanched in
   boiling water for 3 minutes, then
   shocked in ice water)

Yields

4 to 6 servings

Pistachio Vinaigrette for an Autumn-Inspired Salad

This dressing graced our red leaf salad that we conjured up for the Autumn 2006 menu. The salad, which featured roasted pears and grilled green onions over Lolla Rossa lettuce, was so popular that it stayed on the menu throughout the Summer of 2007.

Blending nuts into a salad dressing is tricky. The dressing can quickly become grainy or too thick if you are not careful. In this recipe, I use a simple sherry vinaigrette as the base and suggest adding the crushed pistachios while tossing the salad to leave them crunchy and flavorful.

Directions

1. Preheat the oven to 350 degrees.

2. Spread the pistachios out on a baking sheet.

3. Drizzle a very small amount of oil over the pistachios (about 1 teaspoon) and mix them around to get a very light coat on the nuts.

4. Roast the pistachios for about 4 to 6 minutes until they are toasty and fragrant, but not dark.

   Note: Ovens are very different, so watch the pistachios carefully. They are expensive and burn easily.

5. When cool, crush the pistachios in a food processor and set aside.

6. In a blender, mix all other dressing ingredients together, except the oil (and pistachios) for about 20 seconds to incorporate them.

7. Then, with the blender on low, drizzle in the oil allowing the dressing to slightly emulsify.

8. When ready to serve the salad, toss all of the salad ingredients with an appropriate amount of dressing and pistachios, and serve immediately.

MANGO SALSA

Late winter, Northeast, USA…cold!

So this is the time of year when the days are a gloomy gray, like today; when the cold weather sinks in deep; when it is dark at 4:30 PM, and when we remember just how really cold it gets up here. I know many of you who thrive in this weather, but I know so very many more who do not.

This is the time of year when I drift down to the tropics. I hop a plane when I can, but in my mind I walk the sandy shores that exist only in pages of books like Herman Wouk's *Don't Stop the Carnival,* where I find myself on the terrace of the Gull Reef Club at dusk, sipping martinis with Norman Paperman and Iris Tramm. I dream of the Florida Keys and imagine myself there 75 years ago, before the billboards and T-shirt shops, back to a time when you could catch a Pan Am clipper from Key West to Cuba.

This is the time of year when I walk into my favorite Latin grocery store and it becomes a mini-vacation. I smell the chiles, taste a lime, eat a mango, and float down the tropical waterways in my mind. I think back to the warmth and sunshine of being on a dock, watching boats float by, sipping rum with Kate, watching the sunset, and listening to the sounds of reggae or steel drums. I dream of the paradises I want to visit—the Grenadines, Eleuthera, Los Roques, and the San Blas.

So as I work on our new monthly menu, I find myself wishing for the simple things in life—the sea, sand, sky, and maybe a palm tree if you want to get frivolous. And when food comes to mind, I find I want the simple things sometimes too.

I love to stretch the limits of what can be done with vegetarian cuisine, though there is a dangerous line that gets crossed eventually. It's a line that separates simple good food from over-innovation. I mean, since when did a truffled huitlacoche kumquat salsa ever taste better than a good old mango salsa.

Horizons: New Vegan Cuisine

Putting mango salsa on your menu these days is like doing Cajun food. It's been done and done to death so much that it becomes cliché. It's for the chain restaurants that are trying to catch up with the trends. But mango salsa, in all its clichéd simplicity, is awesome. Just like when Cajun food is done right. The mango is a beautiful fruit. It grows in every tropical climate, and mixes so perfectly well with juicy tomatoes, limes, peppers, and onions to make a vibrantly colorful and delicious salsa. A trend that is as good as it is timeless.

So, I'm done experimenting and wandering the market and daydreaming myself through Mexico. It's mango salsa on the next menu! Why? Because on a gray day like today, it's simply perfect. ▪

APPETIZERS

Ingredients

1 (16-ounce) jar or can unmarinated
    artichokes, drained
1 (12-ounce) can white beans, rinsed
    and drained
½ cup onion, chopped
1 teaspoon fresh garlic, crushed
½ cup green bell pepper, chopped
¼ cup vegan mayo
1 teaspoon black pepper
½ teaspoon salt
1 teaspoon seafood seasoning
1 teaspoon Dijon mustard

Yields
4 servings

Artichoke & White Bean Dip

Here is a great cocktail party dip or filling for tea sandwiches. It makes a great mock tuna salad as well. Remember to keep it coarse so that the wonderful textures stand out.

If you can find greek gigande beans, try them with this recipe. They are huge, creamy, and flavorful. If not, cannelini (white kidney), great northern, and navy beans work well.

Directions

1. Pulse all ingredients in a food processor until coarse and chunky.

2. Chill for at least 30 minutes.

3. Serve with crackers, pita, or mini rye or pumpernickel toast.

   Note: This dip also makes a great sandwich when combined with veggie bacon, tomato, and vegan mayo.

Hongos Rellenas with Vegan Chipotle Sour Cream

One of my first and favorite experiences with Latin food was at a restaurant called Gabriel in Washington, DC. (They have unfortunately since changed their concept). This is where Kate and I had our first mojitos and caipirinhas. It's also where I experienced a truly inspiring collection of flavors—from black bean and plantain empanadas to mushroom croquettes to arepas and stuffed piquillo peppers.

These hongos rellenas (Latin stuffed mushrooms) embody some of the spirit and great flavors of that wonderful experience. If you like more mild foods, substitute smoked paprika for the chipotle in the sour cream ingredients.

Directions

1. Preheat oven to 400 degrees.

2. In a mixing bowl, toss the mushrooms with the 2 tablespoons oil and the salt and pepper, and set aside.

3. Peel the plantain and slice it into 1-inch thick rounds.

4. Sauté the plantain slices in a shallow layer (about 1 tablespoon) of canola oil on medium heat until golden brown. Remove from heat, sprinkle on the Latin Spice blend, and allow to cool.

5. In a food processor, blend the beans, 2 teaspoons canola oil, and cooled plantains until it makes a smooth, thick paste and set aside

   Note: If the mixture is too dry, add a little water.

6. Stuff the mushrooms generously with the plantain-bean paste.

7. Bake the stuffed mushrooms for 12 to 15 minutes or until the mushrooms have softened.

8. Meanwhile, prepare the sour cream by mixing all the ingredients in a small mixing bowl.

9. When the mushrooms come out of the oven, serve with the sour cream drizzled on top or in a ramekin on the side.

Mushroom Ingredients

10 to 12 large white mushroom caps, stems removed
2 tablespoons canola oil to coat the mushrooms
1 teaspoon salt
1 teaspoon pepper

Stuffing Ingredients

1 ripe plantain (should have a nice amount of black on it)
1 tablespoon canola oil for sautéing the plantains and 2 teaspoons for blending with the beans
1 teaspoon Latin Spice blend
1 (12-ounce) can pinto beans, rinsed and drained

Sour Cream Ingredients

1 cup vegan sour cream or vegan mayo
2 teaspoons chipotle powder
Pinch salt

Yields

2 to 4 servings

Marinade Ingredients

2 tablespoons Latin Spice blend
¼ cup olive or canola oil

Appetizer Ingredients

1 very large Italian Eggplant, peeled
    and cut into 1-inch planks
½ cup onion, chopped
1 jalapeno, chopped
1 cup tomatoes, chopped
1 tablespoon pumpkin seed butter
1 teaspoon olive oil
½ cup cilantro leaves
2 tablespoons fresh lime juice
½ teaspoon salt or to taste
Tortilla chips or soft tortillas for wraps
    (optional)

Yields

2 to 4 servings

Mexican Baba Ghanoush

Baba ghanoush is a Mediterranean puree of eggplant with tahini (sesame seed paste), lemon juice, and olive oil, with herbs and other vegetables sometimes added. I was inspired by the idea of the eggplants taking a trip across the Atlantic and washing up on the spicy sunny shores of Mexico.

In this version, I add dimensions of flavor by grilling the eggplant to give it a smokiness, trading the lemon juice for lime juice, and substituting the tahini for a more Mexican touch of pumpkin seed butter (available at ethnic or natural foods markets or online). If you don't want to add the pumpkin seed butter, you may leave it out, since the dish is just as good without it.

I like this salad "pulsed" in the food processor, meaning short bursts to keep things nice and coarse. You can also hand chop everything for a nice rustic look.

Directions

1. Heat grill to medium heat.

2. Mix the marinade ingredients together until well combined.

3. Brush the eggplant planks with the marinade mix.

4. Grill the eggplant on each side until it is soft, approximately 5 to 10 minutes, depending on thickness.

5. Remove eggplant from the grill and place in a mixing bowl.

6. Cover the bowl and let the eggplant rest for at least 15 minutes.

7. Place the eggplant and the rest of the ingredients in a food processor and pulse until the consistence is a nice chunky texture or chop finely by hand.

   Note: You may puree the mixture it if you like, but the little chunks of vegetables really make the texture shine.

8. Chill for at least one hour.

9. Serve the baba ghanoush with tortilla chips or soft tortillas for wraps.

Mexican Baba Ghanoush

EGGPLANT was one of the early icons of vegetarian cooking. Most vegetarian restaurants don't dare put this stuff on their menu. However, when done right, eggplant deserves its place in the spotlight.

Mushroom Ingredients

12 large white mushroom caps, stems removed
2 tablespoons canola oil to coat the mushrooms
1 teaspoon salt
1 teaspoon pepper

Stuffing Ingredients

1 (12-ounce) bag spinach, cleaned
1 cup fennel, chopped
½ cup onion, chopped
1 garlic clove
1 tablespoon Dijon mustard
1 tablespoon vegan mayo
1 teaspoon olive oil
2 teaspoons white wine
1 teaspoon salt
1 teaspoon pepper

Yields

2 to 4 servings

Mushrooms Stuffed with Fennel & Spinach

Classic stuffed mushrooms are a great finger food for cocktail parties. I love to invent funky stuffing ideas for mushrooms. This version is an ode to spring with a French accent. I know many people who say they don't like fennel, usually because they have been overdosed with a heavy-handed use of fennel seed in the past. Fresh fennel is a good way to reintroduce this flavor to the skeptics. It is delicate and subtle, with the added crunch of a fresh vegetable. It's Paris in the Spring time!

Directions

1. Preheat oven to 400 degrees.

2. In a mixing bowl, toss the mushrooms with the 2 tablespoons oil and the salt and pepper, and set aside.

3. In a food processor, puree the stuffing ingredients into a course paste.

4. Stuff the mushrooms and bake for 12 to 15 minutes or until the mushrooms have softened and the filling is dark green and bubbly.

Nori Spring Rolls

Nori is the pressed and dried seaweed sheets most commonly known for making sushi maki rolls. These are a great complement to the Korean Grilled Tofu Steak in this book (page 109). This recipe is more of an "egg roll" type concept, with the nori encasing a shredded vegetable filling. The taste of the nori itself adds such an incredible dimension of flavor to the basic Asian sauce ingredients used to dress the vegetables.

Directions

1. Prepare the finishing sauce by whisking together all sauce ingredients in a small mixing bowl and set aside.

2. In a large wok, heat the teaspoon of canola oil on high heat. When it starts to ripple, gently add the cabbage, carrots, and snow peas by sliding them carefully down the sides of the wok.

3. Stir fry vegetables for 1 to 2 minutes until they just start to turn a bit soft.

   Note: Vegetables that are too crisp will tear the nori when rolled.

4. Next add the spinach, scallions, and ginger to the wok and stir fry for 1 more minute.

5. Add the finishing sauce and let the flavors combine for 1 minute on medium heat.

6. Remove from the burner and let the mixture cool slightly.

7. Divide vegetable mixture into 4 portions and place each portion in the center of a nori sheet.

8. Roll up the sheet as if you were about to roll a burrito—pull the front of the nori over the top of the mixture, then fold in the sides as you finish the roll.

Sauce Ingredients

2 teaspoons tamari soy sauce
1 teaspoon toasted sesame oil
½ teaspoon white pepper
1 teaspoon sugar

Spring Roll Ingredients

1 teaspoon canola oil
3 cups cabbage, shredded
2 cups carrots, shredded
1 cup snow peas, slivered
2 teaspoons ginger, grated or chopped (skin removed)
¼ cup scallions, chopped
1 cup fresh spinach, chopped
4 sheets nori seaweed (buy good quality sheets; the cheap ones crumble as you roll them)

Yields

4 servings

Some guests at the restaurant pause when they read "oyster mushroom" or "lobster mushroom" on our menu, but there is no cause for alarm. The name is only intended to convey a similar flavor profile and appearance to their namesake.

Oyster Mushroom Rockefeller

Oyster Mushroom Rockefeller

You gotta love those classic throwbacks: Veal Oscar, Beef Wellington, Chicken Cordon Bleu, and of course Oysters Rockefeller; however, you also have to ask yourself: "how did these people survive?"

Here's a fun twist on Oysters Rockefeller! Oyster mushrooms alone don't taste exactly like seafood, and I suppose they are named after the mollusk because of their pale gray color. Even this vegan-prepared dish is still wonderfully decadent and indulgent. I like the effect of small, individual portions served as appetizers. A glass of dry, white wine and some oyster crackers (they don't taste like seafood either) go perfectly with this dish.

Mushroom Ingredients

1 (12-ounce) package of fresh oyster mushrooms
2 tablespoons olive oil
1 pound fresh spinach

Sauce Ingredients

1 teaspoon Dijon mustard
¼ cup vegan mayo
3 teaspoons Pernod (Anise liquor)
2 tablespoons olive oil
½ teaspoon salt
½ teaspoon pepper
1 teaspoon crushed garlic
1 teaspoon sugar

Yields

2 to 4 servings

Directions

1. Preheat oven to 400 degrees.

2. Remove and discard any tough parts of the mushroom stems.

3. Layer the mushrooms in the bottom of a small ovenware dish, preferably a gratin or soufflé (or make several individual-sized portions in a smaller baking dish).

4. Heat a large sauté pan and drizzle it with the olive oil.

5. Lightly wilt the spinach by cooking it for about 1 minute, tossing occasionally.

6. Remove wilted spinach from the heat and layer it on top of the mushrooms.

7. Combine the sauce ingredients in a small mixing, then spoon a generous portion on top of the spinach until it is completely covered.

8. Bake for 15 minutes or until the sauce browns lightly.

   Note: The mushrooms can be finished under the broiler to get a nice brown, bubbly top; however, make sure to watch it so it doesn't burn.

Ingredients

2 large burrito-sized tortillas
  (10 to 12 inches in diameter)
12 ounces smoked tofu, chopped
¼ cup red onion, chopped
2 tablespoons capers
2 tablespoons black olives, chopped
2 tablespoons fresh dill leaves,
  chopped
2 small plum tomatoes, chopped
1 cup your favorite vegan cheese or
  spread on some vegan sour cream
2 teaspoons extra virgin olive oil

Yields

2 pizzas or 4 to 6 servings

Tortilla Pizza with Smoked Tofu

Just north of Quebec City in the Saint Lawrence River is Ile d'Orléans, and if it wasn't for the 9-month cold period each year, I would have to count this and Quebec City among the most perfect places I have found in my travels. The island is beautiful and slightly hilly with wonderful river views, open fields, deep forests, great-looking houses, beautiful flowers, and the restaurant in which I plan to retire… someday. Well, only if the climate drastically changes in the next 30 years!

This restaurant was along the main island loop road, a white-washed, cottage-like building at the base of a hill with an outdoor patio and waterfall. I could see myself there, working a few days a week doing classic French country vegetarian cuisine, drinking wine, and having an herb garden. The present chef had other goals—not a vegetarian item on the menu. Even the salad had duck or raccoon on it, or something. So we passed, but I must say that back in Quebec City, we ate some truly wonderful French meals. Here is a Horizons tribute to some great French Cuisine that is not an ocean away.

Directions

1. Preheat oven to 400 degrees.

2. Place tortillas on a baking sheet.

3. Spread all ingredients evenly over both tortillas.

4. Bake for 10 to 12 minutes or until the edges of the tortilla turn brown.

Tortilla Pizza with Smoked Tofu

Taco Ingredients

1 cup dried red lentils
3 ½ cups water
1 tablespoon canola oil
2 tablespoons onion, finely chopped
2 teaspoons Latin Spice blend
4 crispy tostadas (corn tortillas)
Vegan sour cream (optional)
Hot sauce (optional)

Salsa Ingredients

1 (12-ounce) jar nopales (cactus),
  drained
5 plum tomatoes, roughly chopped
½ cup onion chopped
½ cup cilantro leaves
1 teaspoon canola oil
1 teaspoon salt
1 teaspoon pepper
1 jalapeno pepper (optional)

Yields

4 servings

Refried Red Lentil Tostadas with Cactus Salsa

Refried lentils have made many appearances on Horizons menus. They are a lighter, more flavorful alternative to traditional refried beans. The tostadas I recommend here are easily found in some supermarkets and Latin grocery stores. You can make your own too by taking soft corn tortillas and lightly frying them in a pan with a shallow layer of neutral oil. Lastly, the nopales (prickly pear cactus pads) are an acquired taste, and I actually prefer the jarred, pickled ones over fresh (although fresh, when prepared properly, are glorious). To me, the taste sings of Mexico, an authentic and unique flavor that jumps outside the American repertoire for Tex-Mex. Try them at least once!

Directions

1. Sort through the lentils for debris, such as tiny stones.

2. Cook lentils in the water, and simmer for 10 minutes or until softened.

3. Transfer cooked lentils to a plate or mixing bowl to cool and prevent over cooking.

4. Meanwhile, pulse all salsa ingredients in a food processor until chunky, and then refrigerate.

5. In a large nonstick pan, heat a tablespoon of canola oil until very hot.

6. Add the onion and sauté for 1 to 2 minutes, letting it brown.

7. Add the cooled lentils and the spice mix and stir with a wooden spoon or spatula until the mixture becomes thick like refried beans.

   Note: If necessary, add a drop or two of oil or water if the lentil mixture dries up too much.

8. Toss all salsa ingredients in a small mixing bowl.

9. Spread the lentil mixture on each tostada and top with the cactus salsa. Vegan sour cream is an excellent touch here too as well as a splash of hot sauce.

Roasted Cauliflower with Citrus Rémoulade

Cauliflower is an amazing vegetable. Too often paired with broccoli in a frozen vegetable medley, it has a shining identity of its own in my book! I love it raw with dip, boiled with margarine, roasted with herbs and garlic, and mashed with potatoes.

This roasted version is great hot or cold, and the citrus rémoulade—a take on a classic French mayonnaise sauce—adds a blanket of richness on the palate.

Directions

1. Preheat oven to 400 degrees.

2. In a large mixing bowl, toss all the cauliflower ingredients thoroughly.

3. Lay out cauliflower mixture on a baking sheet and bake for about 10 minutes or until the edges of the cauliflower brown.

4. In a medium mixing bowl, gently combine the rémoulade ingredients and refrigerate until chilled.

5. Serve the cauliflower either hot or cold with the chilled rémoulade spooned on top or on the side for dipping.

Cauliflower Ingredients

2 heads of cauliflower, cut into
   1 to 2 inch chunks
2 teaspoons garlic, chopped
½ cup olive oil
Salt and pepper to taste

Rémoulade Ingredients

1 cup vegan mayo
2 teaspoons chopped capers
5 cornichons (French baby pickles),
   finely chopped
¼ cup onion, finely chopped
1 teaspoon fresh lemon juice
1 teaspoon salt
1 teaspoon pepper
2 tablespoons Dijon mustard
1 teaspoon sugar

Yields

2 to 4 servings

Portobella Mushroom Fingers with Creamy Corn & Green Olive Relish

Portobella Mushroom Fingers with Creamy Corn & Green Olive Relish

Here's a great selection for a cocktail party, or better yet, a good dish for kids. Roasted, meaty portobella mushroom fingers pair beautifully with the creamy, multi-flavor dimensions of one of my favorite relishes. In fact, the relish was inspired by an egg salad my mom and I used to make when I was a kid.

Directions

1. Preheat oven to 450 degrees.

2. Cut mushrooms into strips about 2 inches wide.

3. Combine oil, salt, pepper, and balsamic vinegar for marinade.

4. In a mixing bowl, combine marinade and mushrooms and toss.

5. Lay the mushrooms strips on a baking sheet and roast for 7 to 10 minutes or until the mushrooms have softened and are cooked through.

   Note: Cooking times will vary based on the thickness of the portobellas, so keep a watchful eye on them to prevent over baking and drying them out.

6. In a food processor, combine the olives, corn, and onion and pulse to get a rough-and-chunky consistency, but not a puree.

7. In a small mixing bowl, toss the corn mixture with the remaining relish ingredients.

8. When the mushroom strips are ready, serve with the relish.

Mushroom Ingredients

3 to 4 large portobella mushroom caps
½ cup olive or canola oil
1 teaspoon salt
2 teaspoons black pepper
1 tablespoon balsamic vinegar

Relish Ingredients

¼ cup Green Manzanilla olives (stuffed with pimento or unstuffed)
1½ cup corn kernels (thawed if using frozen, or boiled and cut off the cob if using fresh)
¼ cup red onion, chopped
½ teaspoon seafood seasoning
¼ cup vegan mayo
1 teaspoon Dijon mustard
¼ cup plum tomatoes, finely chopped

Yields

4 servings

Bruschetta Ingredients

1 crusty baguette
2 packages store-bought Asian-
 flavored smoked or baked tofu

Relish Ingredients

2 bunches fresh cilantro leaves
½ bunch fresh mint leaves, no stem
8 plum tomatoes, seeds removed
1 clove garlic
1 jalapeno pepper, seeds and
 membrane removed
3 scallion whites, chopped
Salt, pepper and sugar to taste, if
 needed
3 tablespoons olive oil
2 tablespoons fresh lime juice

Red Chile Mayo Ingredients

2 cups vegan mayo
½ cup sriracha (hot chili sauce)
2 tablespoons sambal olek
 (red chili sauce)
1 teaspoon sugar
1 teaspoon salt and black pepper

Yields

4 servings

Vietnamese Bruschetta

Vietnamese culture is emerging strongly in Philadelphia, and there are several of these great little Vietnamese hoagie shops in our area. This is a twist on the classic Vietnamese Tofu Hoagie, which is a long roll slathered with mayo and stuffed with lemon-grass-braised tofu, hot peppers, and fresh cilantro. I have taken a few direction changes to reinvent this sandwich as finger food for a party.

I have recommended buying an Asian-flavored smoked or baked tofu to make this simple. However, if you want, buy regular tofu and simmer it slowly for 10 to 15 minutes in a vegetable stock with about 3 crushed lemon grass stalks and a little tamari. Let it dry and cool before using.

Directions

1. Cut baguette into 1-inch-thick slices. Cover and set side.

2. Cut tofu in pieces that easily fit on top of the bread slices. Refrigerate pieces until ready to assemble.

3. Pulse the tomatoes in the food processor until they are a coarse relish (with no big chunks) and remove from processor to a small mixing bowl.

4. Add all other relish ingredients to food processor and pulse into a fine relish.

(continued next page)

5. Add the finely pulsed relish mixture to the tomatoes and gently mix to combine.

6. Refrigerate the relish mixture for at least 20 minutes before adjusting seasoning, if necessary.

7. Meanwhile, slowly whisk together all red chile mayo ingredients in a medium mixing bowl and refrigerator until ready to serve.

   Note: Mixing too quickly will break up the mayo and make it separate.

8. Just before serving, spread the red chile mayo on the baguette slices, and assemble the tofu and relish on top.

Vietnamese Bruschetta

Cake Ingredients

3 medium potatoes, peeled and
  chopped
¼ cup black olives, chopped
  (kalamata or niçoise work best)
Pinch salt
2 teaspoons black pepper
2 tablespoons olive oil for mashing
4 to 6 tablespoons canola oil for frying

Relish Ingredients

6 plum tomatoes, tops cut off and
  seeds squeezed out
1 bunch basil, large stems removed
¼ cup red onion, chopped
1 teaspoon salt
1 teaspoon black pepper
1 teaspoon extra virgin olive oil
1 teaspoon crushed garlic

Yields

4 to 6 servings

Potato-Black Olive Cakes with Tomato Basil Relish

These wonderful potato cakes have been on the Horizons menu for years as an accompaniment to our Portobella Mushroom Carpaccio. It's not only a great appetizer. You can also make the cakes a base for a reinvented salade niçoise. Serve them with the Garlic Green Beans with Marcona Almonds & Vegan Tarragon Butter (see recipe on page 141) and chopped tomatoes.

Directions

1. Boil the potatoes until tender and then remove from water to cool.

2. When cooled enough to handle, mash the cooked potatoes with the olives, salt, pepper, and olive oil.

3. Refrigerate mashed potatoes or leave in a cool place to set.

4. Lightly pulse the relish ingredients in a food processor until chunky, but not pureed, and then refrigerate.

5. When ready, form the cooled potato mixture into small cakes about 4 to 5 inches wide and about 1 inch thick.

6. Heat a non-stick skillet or flat griddle pan on high heat.

7. Pour about a tablespoon of canola oil in the center of the hot pan.

8. Griddle the first cake on each side, turning with a spatula to flip. It should be golden brown and crisp.

9. Repeat for the remaining cakes.

10. Serve cakes hot with the chilled relish.

Tortilla Pierogies with Truffled Sour Cream

Here is a great cocktail party food idea. They are so easy to prepare and so amazingly delicious. Consider them a cross between a quesadilla and a traditional pierogi. What more could you want?

I prefer to use Yukon gold potatoes for these hors d'oeuvres, but an all-purpose chef's potato will work just as well. Baking potatoes are too starchy for the filling and red-skin or new potatoes are not starchy enough.

If you drink alcohol, these pierogies are perfect with beer. I recommend a nice amber ale.

Directions

1. In a small bowl, mix the truffle oil with the sour cream and refrigerate until ready to use.

2. Begin by bringing about 3 quarts of water to a boil.

3. Add the potatoes and boil until fork tender (anywhere from 8-12 minutes).

4. Drain the potatoes and transfer them to a large bowl with the salt, pepper, and margarine.

5. Mash the potatoes with a potato masher or the back of a large fork until thick and smooth. Adjust the salt and pepper to taste.

6. Lay the tortillas flat and spread a thin even layer (about ¼ inch thick) of potato mixture all over the surface of the tortilla.

7. Fold the tortilla in half.

8. Heat olive oil in a nonstick griddle pan on medium heat (use 1 tablespoon for each tortilla).

9. Add the folded tortilla to the heated oil and sear each side for about 1 minute each, being careful not to let it burn.

10. Once the tortilla is seared to a nice golden brown (it should be slightly crispy), remove it from the pan and cut into 4 or 6 wedges.

11. Repeat with the other tortilla.

12. Top each wedge with a dollop of the sour cream and a sprinkling of chives.

Sour Cream Ingredients

2 teaspoons truffle oil
1 cup vegan sour cream (or vegan mayo)
2 tablespoons fresh chives, chopped, for garnish

Pierogi Ingredients

3 medium sized potatoes, cubed
1 teaspoon salt
1 teaspoon pepper
2 tablespoons margarine (more if you like richer potatoes)
2 (10-inch) flour tortillas
2 tablespoons olive oil for searing the tortillas

Yields

4 to 8 servings as an appetizer or party food

Ingredients

2 (12-ounce) cans chick peas, rinsed
   and drained
2 garlic cloves
½ cup water
1 tablespoon lemon juice
¼ cup olive oil
½ teaspoon salt
1 teaspoon pepper (preferably freshly
   ground)
1 teaspoon fresh thyme leaves
1 dash ground cumin
2 teaspoons quality truffle oil (or more
   as desired)
Optional garnishes include paprika,
   ground chile, or chopped parsley

Yields
4 servings

Truffled Hummus

What could be better than a good hummus? It's a classic, and it makes an easy party food. Making it yourself is only slightly more difficult than opening that store-bought plastic container, yet the result yields a freshness of flavor and a creamy texture that can't be beat.

The use of white truffle oil lends itself well to the earthiness of the ground chick peas. Chips, toasted pita, or fresh cut veggies are a must!

Directions - Option #1

1. In a food processor, blend all ingredients until smooth and creamy.

2. Garnish with a sprinkle of paprika or ground chile for heat, or fresh chopped parsley also makes an outstanding garnish.

Directions - Option #2

1. In a food processor, blend all ingredients except the truffle oil until smooth and creamy.

2. Garnish by drizzling the truffle oil on top, which creates more of a layered taste.

UGLY FOOD

It's mid-November. The leaves are gone and so is any sign that this place was once a warm barefooted, green-shaded playground. The rum is put away, the basil has withered, and the tomato plants are no more. The holidays are beckoning, and it's time to do some real cooking now.

This time of year breeds what I call "ugly food." You know what I mean: the Thanksgiving table spread, the over-baked casseroles, the things that have been roasted all day, the murky brown gravy, the gray mushy stuffing. Ugly!

Thanksgiving is comfort food in the extreme for Americans. On Thanksgiving Day, we get sentimental and traditional and we overeat ugly food. There is no need to go to extremes to fix it. You don't need to top your veggie loaf or seitan roast with mango salsa. You also don't need to splash around beet vinaigrettes and set up honeydew boats.

Here are a few tips to wake up your vegetarian Thanksgiving feast. But first and foremost, give thanks. None of us have everything we want in life, but if for one day we would stop subjecting ourselves to advertising, stop looking at the new toys our neighbors have, forget about the American pressures to become bigger, better, faster, stronger; and just look around our own home, we will find so much for which to be thankful. You have more than you think in life, and Thanksgiving is a great day to recognize it.

Now, back to the food...

- **Don't overcook your vegetables!** That is a felony where I come from. If you want to prepare your green vegetables ahead of time, blanch them in boiling water until they turn a bright vibrant green, and then immediately shock them in ice water. This will set the color, and they will only need a slight reheating when you are ready for dinner. Broccoli, broccolini, and broccoli rabe as well as asparagus and kale take to this process very well.

- **Don't forget your fresh herbs!** We don't live in the arctic. There are actually things still growing this time of year, especially thyme and rosemary. These perfect autumn flavors can help us celebrate with dramatic garnishes for the table.

- **Serve some fresh, marinated vegetable salads with dinner!** This will help cut the richness of the comfort foods and give the palate a refreshing change of texture. Try some baby carrots marinated with crushed garlic, salt, olive oil, and red wine vinegar (start them the night before for best results). Or try some cucumbers with chopped dill, salt, and crushed coriander seeds. Better yet, try a shredded radish salad with a touch of rice wine vinegar, salt, pepper, and a pinch of sugar.

- **Don't be afraid of a few tropical touches!** Florida, California, New Mexico, and Hawaii are still part of the United States the last time I checked; and Puerto Rico and the Virgin Islands are not far behind. How about having an avocado and fresh spinach salad? Try some boniato instead of sweet potatoes. Boniato is a Cuban sweet potato found all over in Florida, and it's making its way north. I don't like sweet potatoes, but I do love boniato. It's incredible, and there's nothing quite like it. Some poblano peppers would wake up any dish, and try calabaza, a west Indian pumpkin squash similar to butternut squash. It's incredible in pumpkin pie or roasted as a dinner vegetable. And guess where all those "pumpkin spices," such as allspice and nutmeg, come from? Yes, the tropics!

- **Try to relax and enjoy yourself!** And most of all, to the 364-day-a-year vegetarians on the fence and the flexitarians who fold to temptation, without sounding preachy, try to go veg this year. There are so many great products out on the market and so many great things you can do with vegetables, it's natural and so easy to give it a try. Plus, I will be checking up on each and every one of you. ▪

ENTRÉES

Ingredients

24 ounces balsamic vinegar
6 ounces agave syrup
3 teaspoons tamari soy sauce
1 tablespoon canola oil
16 ounces seitan, drained and rinsed

Yields

2 to 3 servings

Balsamic & Agave Glazed Seitan

This seitan dish predated the BBQ seitan at Horizons Café. A lot of people said it reminded them of spareribs at a Chinese restaurant. The ingredients are simple and so is the preparation once you get the vinegar reduced. The sauce keeps for a very long time in the refrigerator, and this is a great recipe to make for first-time seitan eaters, especially if you are using small bits of seitan.

Balsamic vinegars vary greatly. If you feel your sauce is too acidic or sour when it reduces, feel free to adjust the amount of agave used. Agave is a fructose-rich nectar from the blue agave cactus plant. It has a really interesting sweet flavor and yet is easy on the bloodstream as far as sugars go. I love working with it.

For an Asian touch, add a dash or two of Five Spice Powder. For a Caribbean touch, pour in ¼ cup of dark rum while the vinegar is reducing.

Directions

1. Pour the vinegar into a medium saucepot and bring to a boil, then reduce the heat to medium-low and let the vinegar reduce by 2/3. This will take anywhere from 25 minutes to an hour, depending on the vinegar, pot, and stove. When it looks like it has thickened, dip a spoon in the vinegar. It should just coat the back of a spoon.

2. Add the agave syrup and tamari, stir and remove from heat.

3. If the sauce gets really thick as it cools, then just add a bit of water (1 tablespoon at a time) to loosen it. At room temperature, it should be the consistency of molasses.

4. When ready, heat oil in a thin wok or griddle pan until it starts to ripple.

5. Add the seitan and brown it on each side.

6. Drizzle the balsamic sauce over the browned seitan and let it coat and caramelize around the seitan, turning the seitan in the pan as needed to coat all sides (about 2 to 4 minutes).

Balsamic & Agave Glazed Seitan

Pesto Ingredients

2 cups fresh basil leaves (lightly packed when measuring)
2 cloves garlic
¼ cup pine nuts
½ teaspoon salt
½ teaspoon pepper
1 tablespoon olive oil
2 tablespoons water

Risotto Ingredients

1 tablespoon olive oil
4 cups cold, precooked basmati rice (prepared according to package directions)
3 cups vegetable stock
1 cup frozen peas
1 cup plum tomatoes, diced
½ teaspoon salt (or adjust to taste)
½ teaspoon pepper
2 tablespoons margarine

Note: I recommend soaking the basmati rice for 20 minutes and rinsing it thoroughly before cooking it in fresh water. Spread out on a baking sheet to cool.

Yields

4 servings

Basmati Risotto with Pesto, Peas & Tomatoes

This is a wonderful, simple, and warming dish that uses aromatic basmati rice to create a rich, flavorful risotto without the hassle of constantly stirring and watching the traditional Arborio rice.

Don't let the light list of ingredients fool you. This recipe prepares an ample entrée, but if you need more "stuff," then try adding some diced zucchini and chopped mushrooms. However, be mindful not to crowd the dish; too many ingredients may detract from the smooth, simple beauty of the aromatic rice.

Directions

1. Pulse all pesto ingredients in a food processor until it forms a rough paste and set aside.

2. To begin the risotto, heat a large pan on medium heat and add the 1 tablespoon of olive oil.

3. When the oil starts to ripple, add the rice.

4. Stir the rice, then add the stock and peas.

5. Stir again, then add the tomatoes. Reduce to low heat.

6. Add the salt, pepper, and margarine, stir until all the margarine is melted and combined.

7. Add the pesto and stir until evenly distributed and serve immediately.

Chilaquiles with Scrambled Tofu & Vegetarian Ground Beef

One morning in Playa del Carmen, Mexico, after a night of tequila sampling, Kate and I sat down to breakfast by the beach. I love Mexican food for breakfast, so I was really excited when the server placed a big plate of a tortilla-like casserole called "chilaquiles" in front of me. I took a big blind hungry bite, and, of course, there was pork in it. As if the hangover wasn't enough!

I came home and did some research. Sure enough, chilaquiles are made by soaking old tortilla chips in pork or chicken stock and then baking them with sauce and cheese. I thought it was a cool concept (everyone has stale chips around at some point, like after Cinqo de Maya or the Super Bowl). And so a new vegetarian brunch idea was born. Once you finish the prep, this dish is hands-free as it just needs to bake in the oven. For a shortcut, feel free to buy a Mexican enchilada sauce at the market instead of making the sauce from scratch. This can serve as an authentic breakfast or an exotic alternative to more familiar Italian lasagna.

Directions

1. Preheat oven to 400 degrees.

2. Simmer the sauce ingredients in a small saucepan over medium-low heat for 15 to 20 minutes. Add water or vegetable stock it if gets too thick.

3. In a large sauté pan, heat the canola oil on medium-high.

4. Sauté the onions and peppers for 5 minutes.

5. Add the tofu and spices and sauté for 5 minutes. If tofu begins to stick, add a touch of water.

6. In a large casserole dish, layer the tortilla chips and cover with half of the sauce.

7. Add the tofu on top, followed by the rest of the sauce and optional cheese.

8. Bake covered for 25 minutes or until the sauce is bubbly.

Sauce Ingredients

1 (12-ounce) can crushed tomatoes (not puree)
3 tablespoons Latin Spice blend
1 (12-ounce) package vegetarian ground beef (or 2 crumbled veggie burgers)
2 tablespoons hot sauce
5 cups old tortilla chips
2 cups vegan cheese (optional)
3½ cups vegetable stock

Tofu Ingredients

2 tablespoons canola oil
½ cup onion, chopped
½ cup bell pepper, chopped
16 ounces tofu, crushed to rough chunks
1 teaspoon turmeric
2 teaspoons Latin Spice blend
Salt and pepper to taste

Yields

2 to 4 servings

Cuban Paella

Cuban Paella

Paella is another one of those great dishes of the world. Hailing from Spain, the original is a vegetarian minefield of sausage, shellfish, and chicken. In this recipe, we will clean it up and take it on a trip across the Atlantic. Cuba has such a strong Spanish background, so it's easy to transition this dish.

Although this is not a traditionally prepared paella, which is made like risotto by stirring in stock as you go with layers of ingredients, the results are fantastic with much less work. Included in this recipe is the authentic Cuban ingredient mentioned earlier in this book—Calabaza. The way it "melts" into this dish with the tomatoes and saffron is incredible.

This dish requires a lot of ingredients, but you can simplify it if you wish. For instance, the paella can be just as sumptuous in an all-vegetable version without the tofu and seitan! Regardless of how you choose to prepare it, this dish is a wonderfully elegant dinner. Enjoy it with some Rioja from Spain and some pressed Cuban bread from a Latin grocery store!

Directions

1. In a very large pot, heat the 2 tablespoons of oil on medium-high heat until the oil starts to ripple.

2. Add the onions, garlic, and bell pepper. Sauté for 3-5 minutes.

3. Add the calabaza and tomatoes and sauté for another 2 minutes.

4. In a separate pan, brown the tofu and seitan with the tablespoon of oil and then add to the main pan with the rest of the ingredients.

5. Cover and simmer for 15 minutes on medium-low heat.

6. When done, stir in the rice, letting all the ingredients incorporate. If it becomes too dry and sticky, add more stock to your liking.

Ingredients

2 tablespoons olive or canola oil to sauté vegetables and 1 tablespoon to brown seitan and tofu

1 large onion, slivered or sliced

4 cloves garlic, crushed

1 green bell pepper, diced

4 cups calabaza, peeled, seeded, and diced

8 plum tomatoes diced

16 ounces tofu, chopped into small dice

16 ounces seitan, drained, rinsed, and chopped

¼ cup manzanilla olives, sliced

¼ cup white wine

1 cup vegetable stock (use a bit more if the rice is very absorbent)

2 teaspoons salt

2 teaspoons pepper

2 teaspoons dried thyme

4 cups rice, precooked jasmine or basmati rice with ¼ teaspoon saffron (prepared according to package directions)

Note: I recommend soaking the rice for 20 minutes and rinsing it thoroughly before cooking it in fresh water. Spread out on a baking sheet to cool.

Yields

4 to 6 servings

Mojo Ingredients

4 cloves garlic, crushed
3 tablespoons fresh lime juice
2 tablespoons olive oil (not extra
    virgin)
1½ teaspoons salt
2 teaspoons pepper
1 teaspoon sugar
2 tablespoons chopped fresh parsley

Tofu Ingredients

Tofu Spice blend for coating tofu
    (see page 15)
1 (16-ounce) block of tofu, cut into
    3 equal slabs
1 large onion, slivered or cut into
    strips
2 teaspoons canola oil

Yields

2 to 3 servings

Cuban Pan-Seared Tofu with Onions & Mojo

This is a simple Cuban pan-fried tofu with lots of onion. The beauty of the dish comes from the mojo that gets added at the last minute. Traditionally, mojo is a simple combination of sour orange juice, garlic, and olive oil. I have recommended more readily available fresh lime juice for this recipe.

Anyone who has eaten at any of the little Cuban cafés in and around Miami knows that the food is simple and complimented by lots of garlic and citrus. We make it a point to have a Cuban feast each time we are in Southeast Florida. Our table is filled with small plates of yucca frita, black beans and rice, avocado salad, papas fritas, tostones, and maduros. And, of course, there is plenty of mojo for dipping! This dish is great served with any of the above-mentioned sides. White rice or quinoa also makes a great starch.

Directions

1. In a small saucepan on very low heat, make the mojo by combining the garlic, lime juice, olive oil, salt, pepper, sugar, and parsley. Let it come up to a light simmer for 2 to 3 minutes, and then remove from heat.

2. Pan-sear the tofu as shown on page 15 of the *In Your Kitchen* section.

3. In a large skillet, heat the canola oil on high heat until it starts to ripple.

4. Add the onions and sauté them for about 2 to 5 minutes, until they begin to brown.

5. Continue cooking onions for about 5 minutes, then remove from heat and allow to cool for 2 to 3 minutes.

6. Pour the mojo mixture into the skillet containing the onions.

7. Place the tofu on a plate and spoon the onion mixture over it.

Cuban Pan-Roasted Tofu with Onions & Mojo

Ingredients

1 tablespoon canola oil
1 large onion, slivered
2 large carrots, peeled and chopped
2 tablespoons garlic, crushed
1 tablespoon fresh ginger, peeled and
   finely chopped
2 tablespoons quality curry powder
16 ounces seitan, drained and rinsed
4 plum tomatoes, chopped
1 green bell pepper, diced
1 cup vegetable stock
1 cup coconut milk
1 teaspoon dried thyme
1 teaspoon allspice, ground
1 dash cinnamon
1 tablespoon brown sugar
Salt and pepper to taste
1 scotch bonnet (habanero) pepper,
   finely chopped (optional for those
   who like spicy!)

Yields

2 to 3 servings

Spicy Jamaican Curry Seitan Stew

I love Caribbean curries! Curry was brought over to the islands by the Indian indentured servants after slavery was abolished. It's just another crazy tale of how the Caribbean's melting pot of culture, music, and food came together. As big countries fought over these islands, and the islands changed hands and eventually gained independence, the marks of different cultures were left behind. And all the while, they cooked!

When curry made its way to Jamaica, the world was treated to one of the all-time great food marriages. Jamaicans create their curries with curry powder, native allspice, cinnamon, thyme, and hot, hot pepper, then simmer it with coconut milk. What else is there to say, but "Welcome to the islands!"

This dish is a must over white or brown rice. Splash a little dark rum in at the last minute if you like, but certainly serve it with fresh lime and maybe a bit of chopped mango.

Directions

1. In a large pot, heat the canola oil over medium heat.

2. Add the onion and brown for 3 to 5 minutes, and then stir in the carrot, garlic, and ginger.

3. Stir in the curry powder and let it become fragrant in the oil without scorching (about 1 to 2 minutes).

4. Add the stock next to keep the curry from scorching.

5. Add the rest of the ingredients and stir to combine.

6. Cover the pot and simmer for 20 to 25 minutes on low heat, stirring occasionally.

7. Before serving, adjust salt and pepper to taste.

Cioppino with Saffron & Fennel

Cioppino was created in San Francisco by homesick Italians. This is a classic dish of pasta and seafood in a brothy tomato sauce. I love taking standbys like this and cleaning them up for a vegetarian-friendly feast.

The addition of fennel and saffron in this recipe gives it a nice, old-country Mediterranean touch, and when the wine and garlic join the party, we are in full-blown pasta heaven. The smell of this sauce will fill your kitchen with enchanting aromas. I recommend taking the whole cooking pot out to the center of the table, just after you've stirred in the basil. A simple salad and loaf of sourdough are all you will ever need this night.

Directions

1. Begin by heating the canola oil in a large pot on medium-high heat. As the oil starts to ripple, drop in the onions and bell peppers and stir.

2. One minute later, add the garlic and sauté the mixture for 3 to 5 minutes until the onion browns.

3. Next, add the tofu and TSP and stir until combined.

4. Add the wine and wait one minute, then add the stock and stir.

5. Next add all the other ingredients, except the fennel, pasta, basil, and extra virgin olive oil.

6. Cover and simmer for 15 minutes on medium-low heat, stirring occasionally.

7. Add the fennel and precooked pasta, and simmer an additional 3 to 5 minutes.

8. Remove from heat and stir in the basil and extra virgin olive oil and serve immediately.

Ingredients

2 tablespoons canola oil
1 medium onion, sliced
1 red bell pepper, diced
4 cloves garlic, crushed
1 (16-ounce) block of tofu, cut into small cubes (or, if you have time, pre-grill tofu according to the *Grilled Tofu Provençale* on page 90)
½ cup textured soy protein (TSP) granules
½ cup white wine
1½ cups vegetable stock
12 plum tomatoes, chopped
Pinch saffron threads
1 teaspoon dried oregano
2 teaspoons salt
2 teaspoons black pepper
Pinch sugar if tomatoes aren't very ripe
1 small fennel bulb, white part only, slivered very finely
1½ pound precooked pasta of your choice (ready at room temperature)
1 cup fresh basil, chopped
1 tablespoon extra virgin olive oil

Yields
4 servings

WHEN ROASTING PORTOBELLAS, save that flavorful stock left in the roasting pan, and use it in the Seitan Beef, Barley & Ale Soup recipe found on page 40.

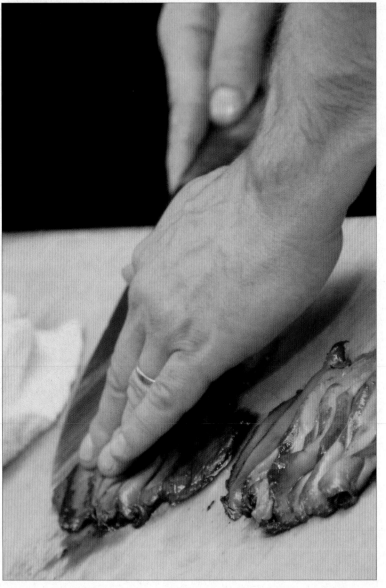

Grilled Portobella Verde Tacos

Grilled Portobella Verde Tacos

A true taco in Mexico is a soft, corn tortilla folded with a filling and topped with cabbage and maybe some sour cream. These hard, crunchy, crumbly things we grew up with are more of a Tex-Mex creation.

Tomatillos, which are giant green berries that look like tomatoes, are an essential part of this salsa verde. Beneath their delicate leaves and thick green skin, they pack a strong sour punch. We balance that tartness with sweetener and salt. If you can't find tomatillos fresh at your supermarket, you may be able to find a quality jarred salsa that lists tomatillos in the ingredients.

However precisely you follow this recipe, remember to keep the limes fresh and the tequila aged. Don't try it the other way around!

Directions

1. Preheat grill to high.

2. Mix the marinade ingredients and use your hands or a brush to completely coat the portobella caps with the marinade.

3. Depending on their size, grill the portobellas on high heat for about 3 to 5 minutes on each side. Don't worry if they seem slightly under-cooked when you pull them from the grill. Place mushrooms on a plate, and they will continue to cook (this is called carry-over cooking) and release their juices.

   Note: Save the juices and use it for incredible mushroom stock.

4. While the mushrooms are cooling, combine the salsa verde ingredients in a food processor, pulsing for about 1 minute.

5. Pour the salsa over the mushrooms and let set a few minutes.

6. In a non-stick fry or griddle pan, heat a small drizzle of oil on medium heat and lightly warm the tortillas on each side for 15 seconds.

7. Slice the portobella caps into strips, and wrap them in the tortillas with additional condiments.

Mushroom & Marinade Ingredients

4 large portobella mushroom caps
⅓ cup canola oil
2 tablespoons balsamic vinegar
1 teaspoon black pepper

Salsa Verde Ingredients

5 tomatillos, outer husk removed
½ onion, chopped
2 garlic cloves
1 green bell or poblano pepper
1 large bunch fresh cilantro, leaves only
1 teaspoon salt
1 teaspoon pepper
2 teaspoons sugar or agave syrup
1 tablespoon canola oil

Tortillas & Taco Condiments

Drizzle canola oil to heat tortillas
4 soft corn tortillas
Avocado slices
Chopped tomatoes, tossed with salt
Shredded cabbage
Vegan sour cream
Sliced jalapeno (optional)

Yields

2 to 4 servings

Tofu & Marinade Ingredients

1 (16-ounce) block of tofu, cut into
   3 equal slabs
¼ cup olive or canola oil
2 tablespoons tamari soy sauce
1 teaspoon black pepper

Sauce Ingredients

2 teaspoons canola oil
4 cloves garlic, crushed
½ cup leek or onion, chopped
¼ cup white wine
1 cup vegetable stock
4 plum tomatoes, diced
½ cup pitted black olives of your
   choice (niçoise olives are best, but
   kalamata or oil-cured olives will
   work fine)
2 teaspoons capers
1 teaspoon Dijon mustard
½ teaspoon salt
½ teaspoon black pepper
1 tablespoon extra virgin olive oil
2 teaspoons fresh thyme

Yields

2 to 3 servings

Grilled Tofu Provençale

The train ride from Antibes to Monaco is a storybook scene of postcards floating by your window, briefly vanishing behind trees or tunnels, only for the next vision to unfold. On my right, I look for little open-air bars and produce markets down by the coast; and to my left, I gaze up hillsides, looking for the village scene where Carey Grant visited his grandmother in "An Affair to Remember."

In the South of France, we ate good, and we ate often. Here is a tribute to all things Provençale! By pre-grilling, we introduce some incredible texture to the tofu, and the big secret is that this dish is ever better served cold, the next day!

Directions

1. Whisk together the marinade ingredients and cover the tofu with the marinade for at least 1 hour, preferably overnight.

2. Grill each side of tofu on high for about 2 to 3 minutes, being careful not to let it char too much, but look for nice, dark brown grill marks.

3. Cool the tofu in the refrigerator.

4. To make the sauce, heat canola oil in a very large sauté pan on high heat until it ripples slightly.

5. Add the leek or onion and garlic and let them brown lightly, about 2 to 4 minutes.

6. Remove the pan from heat to add the white wine, and then return it to the heat for 1 minute.

7. Add the stock, tomatoes, olives, capers, mustard, salt and pepper, and stir together to combine.

8. Just before serving, add the cooled tofu from the refrigerator.

9. Allow the whole dish to simmer for about 5 minutes, enough to heat the tofu through.

10. Finish by adding the fresh thyme and extra virgin olive oil.

11. Serve over plain potatoes, rice or some lightly cooked spinach.

Horizons: New Vegan Cuisine

Grilled Tofu Provençale

Ingredients

2 teaspoons canola oil
½ large head cauliflower, florets
    separated
3 garlic cloves, chopped
½ cup white wine
1 cup vegetable stock
Pinch saffron threads
2 cups Israeli (toasted) couscous,
    cooked according to package in-
    structions (usually 8 to 10 minutes),
    rinsed in cold water and drained
4 plum tomatoes, chopped
½ cup Moroccan oil-cured olives,
    pitted and chopped
1 teaspoon salt
1 teaspoon pepper
1 bulb fennel, slivered, grated or finely
    chopped
1½ tablespoons extra virgin olive oil
Fresh basil leaves (for garnish)

Yields

4 servings

Israeli Couscous with Saffron, Olives, Fennel & Cauliflower

Israeli couscous are large tapioca-sized pearls of pasta, very much unlike traditional tiny grains of couscous. In fact, they have nothing similar about them except that they are both pastas. Israeli couscous has a slippery, silky, almost buttery texture that takes well to so many sauces.

This dish is a light and aromatic stew that will carry you deep into the Mediterranean and to the north shores of Africa. Use whatever black olives you like, but Moroccan oil-cured olives are the best. Exotic and mysterious, they add a deep, salty, sweet flavor. For olive lovers, once you've tried them, you will have a new favorite!

Directions

1. In a large sauté pan, heat the canola oil over medium-high heat until rippling.

2. Add the cauliflower and garlic, and let it lightly brown for about 3 to 5 minutes.

3. Deglaze the pan with the white wine and let it reduce for 1 minute, and then add the stock.

4. Add the saffron, couscous, tomatoes, olives, salt, and pepper.

5. Let the flavors come together and the liquid absorb for about 5 minutes.

6. Spoon into serving bowls and top each with portions of the fennel, extra virgin olive oil, and fresh basil.

Korean Grilled Tofu Steak

Another item on my ever-growing list of favorite products is kochujang, which is a Korean, fermented bean paste with chiles and hot peppers. It comes in different degrees of heat—just read the ingredients and see where "hot pepper" lands in the order. My favorite, by far, is the version that lists hot pepper first and is usually packaged in a red container.

If you ever have had dolsot bibimbap in a Korean restaurant (a sizzling clay pot full of sticky rice and searing vegetables—don't forget to request without the meat!), you will be already familiar with kochujang. It is the hot red sauce served on the side to accompany this magical dish. Try it once and you will have a new obsession!

This dish is great served with steamed or fried rice and an Asian green vegetable.

Tofu & Marinade Ingredients

1 (16-ounce) block of tofu, cut into 3 equal slabs
¼ cup tamari soy sauce
¼ cup canola oil
1 teaspoon white pepper

Sauce Ingredients

¼ cup canola oil
¼ cup toasted sesame oil
¼ cup kochujang (red chile bean paste)
1 teaspoon white pepper
2 tablespoons ginger, skin removed and grated or minced
1 garlic clove
2 tablespoons sugar
Approximately 1 tablespoon water

Yields

2 to 3 servings

Directions

1. Whisk together the marinade ingredients and cover the tofu with the marinade for at least 1 hour, preferably overnight.

2. Preheat the grill to high.

3. Meanwhile, in a blender, combine all sauce ingredients until smooth.

4. Grill each side of tofu on high for about 2 to 3 minutes, being careful not to let it char too much, but look for nice, dark brown grill marks.

5. Once flipped, brush the top of the tofu with the kochujang sauce mixture.

6. Let the sauce absorb for a minute and then remove the tofu from the grill.

Island Mango BBQ Tempeh with Chayote Slaw

Island Mango BBQ Tempeh with Chayote Slaw

Tempeh is one of the most-feared substances in the vegetarian world. Granted, its texture takes some getting used to. This is a soy product made from fermented whole soybeans, and I believe that the key to good tempeh comes from a three-stage process. It's extra work, but I think the results are well worth the effort. By first boiling the tempeh (you could steam it if you prefer), we open it up so that we can get flavor all the way through it. Then by roasting it, we get a nice spice crust layer. Finally, the BBQ sauce provides an exceptional sticky, sweet finish. The chayote slaw is a great accompaniment. Chayote is a squash-like fruit about the size of a mango, which has a mild, fresh flavor and a crunchy texture ideal for a slaw-style salad.

Tempeh & Marinade Ingredients

1 (12 to 16 ounce) slab of tempeh, cut into 2 blocks
¼ cup canola oil
2 tablespoons Latin Spice blend
1 cup ketchup
3 tablespoons molasses
¼ cup mango, skinned, pitted, and cut into chunks
¼ cup water

Slaw Ingredients

1 chayote, pitted
1 carrot, peeled
½ head white cabbage
1 bunch scallions, chopped finely
1 teaspoon salt
1 teaspoon sugar
1 teaspoon rice wine vinegar
1 teaspoon pepper
2 tablespoons fresh lime juice
1 tablespoon canola oil

Yields

2 servings

Note: Chayotes have a small, white oval pit that is actually edible when cooked.

Tempeh Directions

1. Preheat oven to 400 degrees.

2. Boil the tempeh in salted water for 5 minutes, and then remove it from the water to cool.

3. In a bowl, mix the oil and Latin Spice blend and rub it onto the cooled tempeh.

4. Place the tempeh on a sheet pan and bake for 7 minutes, turning once halfway through.

5. Next, blend all of the other marinade ingredients together.

6. When the tempeh is finished baking, coat it with the sauce and bake for an additional 2 to 3 minutes.

Slaw Directions

1. Using the shredder blade of a food processor or a box grater, shred the vegetables and place them in a large mixing bowl.

2. In a small mixing bowl, combine the salt, sugar, vinegar, pepper, lime juice, and oil to create a slaw vinaigrette.

3. Drizzle the vinaigrette over the vegetables, toss thoroughly, and allow slaw to chill for at least 45 minutes.

4. Serve with the BBQ tempeh.

Tempeh & Vegetable Ingredients

1 (12 to 16 ounce) slab of tempeh, cut into 2 blocks
2 teaspoons canola oil
1 onion, cut into strips
1 carrot, peeled and cut into ½ inch wheels
1 stalk celery, cut into 1 inch pieces
3 cups nappa or white cabbage, shredded

Marinade Ingredients

2 tablespoons tamari soy sauce
2 tablespoons canola oil
1 teaspoon white pepper
2 teaspoons red chile paste

Sauce Ingredients

1 cup vegetable stock
1 cup coconut milk
¼ cup peanut butter
2 tablespoons ginger, peeled and chopped
2 garlic cloves, chopped
2 tablespoons sugar
1 tablespoon canola oil
2 teaspoons curry paste (substitute curry powder if necessary)

Yields

2 servings

Malaysian Tempeh

Here's another tempeh recipe that's a bit more involved. Because the tempeh is made of compressed soy beans, I feel it is an excellent compliment to Thai or Malaysian food. The combination of curry and coconut milk with the nutty flavor of the soy beans makes a perfect Southeast Asian, tropical harmony.

Use the vegetables I have recommended or use what you like. For a shortcut, try cutting the tempeh into chunks and putting it right into the stir fry. This dish is delicious over white or brown rice, but even better with pad thai noodles.

Directions

1. Preheat oven to 400 degrees.

2. Boil the tempeh in salted water for 5 minutes.

3. Remove the tempeh from the water and allow it to cool to room temperature.

4. Meanwhile, in a small mixing bowl, combine the marinade ingredients and set aside.

5. In another small mixing bowl, combine the sauce ingredients and set aside.

6. When the tempeh is cool to the touch, rub the marinade on and bake the tempeh on a sheet pan for 7 to 8 minutes. Then lower the oven temperature to 200 degrees to keep warm.

7. In a wok or large sauté pan, heat the oil until it almost reaches the smoking point.

8. Gently drop the vegetables into the hot wok or pan and toss around with tongs or a wok spatula.

9. When the vegetables start to brown slightly, add the sauce and heat for another 4 to 5 minutes or until the sauce comes to a light simmer.

10. Serve the tempeh on top of the vegetables and pour extra sauce on top.

Pasta Sheets with Mushrooms, Red Wine & Rosemary

Living near south Philadelphia and the Italian market, the side streets are lined with Mom & Pop restaurants. Aromas of tomato gravy and garlic waft through the air. There's so much history around here, and it is delicious.

When you are craving a simple, comfort food, this recipe does wonders. The deeply flavored pasta will appeal to anyone who can appreciate simple miracles, like the melding of mushrooms, garlic, and wine. And the fresh rosemary infuses the sauce with a haunting woodsy tone.

You can buy pasta sheets, but in a pinch, I use lasagna and break it off into squares before cooking.

Ingredients

- 2 teaspoons canola oil
- ¼ cup shallot, leek, or onion, chopped
- 2 tablespoons garlic, crushed
- 1½ pounds white or crimini mushrooms, brushed clean of dirt and sliced
- ½ cup red wine of your choice
- 1 cup vegetable stock
- ½ teaspoon salt or less to taste
- ½ teaspoon black pepper
- 2 large sprigs of rosemary
- ½ pound pasta sheets or broken lasagna noodles, precooked according to package instructions and then shocked in cold running water (drizzle a little oil on noodles after they drain to keep them from sticking)
- 2 tablespoons margarine

Directions

1. In a large skillet or pot, heat the oil on high heat until it ripples.

2. Add the shallot and garlic and stir.

3. Add the sliced mushrooms on top of the shallot and garlic.

4. Let the shallot and garlic lightly brown (about 3 to 5 minutes), then add the red wine.

5. Simmer for 2-3 minutes to reduce the wine by half, then add the stock, salt, and pepper.

6. While simmering the stock on low, add the rosemary sprigs.

7. Remove the rosemary after 3 minutes or when it turns dark green (leaving the rosemary in too long will make the dish bitter).

8. Add the precooked pasta and the margarine.

9. Let the pasta absorb some sauce while the margarine melts. When fully melted, the dish is done.

Yields

4 servings

Ingredients

1 tablespoon canola oil
1 medium red onion, sliced
2 cloves garlic, crushed
2 (16-ounce) cans hearts of palm
   (unmarinated, drained, and roughly
   chopped into rounds)
½ cup vegetable stock
4 plum tomatoes, diced
1 (12-ounce) can coconut milk
1 tablespoon sugar
2 teaspoons Latin Spice blend
1 green pepper of your choice
   (green bell, jalapeno or poblano, or
   habanero, depending on desired
   spiciness)
½ cup fresh cilantro leaves (lightly
   packed when measuring)
Lime wedges for garnish

Yields

2 to 3 servings

Hearts of Palm Moqueca

Moqueca is a classic Brazilian dish—both spicy and sweet. It is traditionally made with seafood. Anyone who has ever read our menu knows about my love of hearts of palm. It's a shame that many people have only ever experienced them in salads. I think they are great sautéed, grilled, baked, or stewed. The texture they take on in a dish like this will really surprise you—especially swimming in the tropical flavors or lime, coconut, and hot pepper. To be as authentic as possible with this recipe, use malagueta peppers (dried) if you can find them.

Directions

1. Begin by heating the oil over medium-high heat in a large skillet or pot.

2. When the oil begins to ripple (after about 1 minute), add the onion and garlic and stir.

3. Add the hearts of palm and brown the mixture for 2 to 4 minutes.

4. Next add the vegetable stock and bring to a boil.

5. Add the tomatoes, coconut milk, sugar, spice, and peppers.

6. Simmer for 5 to 10 minutes on medium-low heat until the tomatoes have just started to break down.

7. Remove from heat and stir in the cilantro.

8. Squeeze the fresh lime wedges on just before eating.

Hearts of Palm Moqueca

Oven-Roasted Tofu with Hawaiian Pesto

One of my favorite experiences in Hawaii was on Kauai, in a little restaurant that featured tofu with an incredible Asian green sauce and pickled ginger. I savored every luscious bite, wishing I could run to my kitchen to experiment. When we finally arrived back in the continental United States, I created this vibrant green pesto, spiked with fresh ginger and macadamia nuts.

Like a lot of our tofu dishes, this one is just as good cold as it is hot. As an entrée, serve it with rice cooked with some coconut milk and a marinated tomato salad. The dish is also great with noodles tossed with diced tomatoes, garlic, and oil.

Tofu & Marinade Ingredients

1 (16-ounce) block of tofu, cut into
   3 equal slabs
2 teaspoons toasted sesame oil
3 tablespoons Latin Spice blend
2 tablespoons tamari soy sauce
¼ cup canola oil

Pesto Ingredients

¼ cup canola oil
2 cups fresh basil leaves (loosely
   packed)
⅓ cup macadamia nuts
1 cup fresh cilantro leaves
   (loosely packed)
2 cloves garlic
2 tablespoons fresh ginger, peeled
   and chopped
¼ cup water

Yields

3 servings

Directions

1. Whisk together the marinade ingredients and cover the tofu with the marinade for at least 1 hour, preferably overnight.

2. Preheat oven to 400 degrees.

3. Bake the marinated tofu for 12 minutes in the oven, then remove and let cool.

4. Meanwhile, make the finishing sauce by pureeing the pesto ingredients in a food processor.

5. Reheat the tofu in the oven for about 2 to 3 minutes until warmed through.

6. When ready to serve, pour the pesto on top.

Shredded Seitan Burrito with Chipotle Sauce

This burrito comes right from the winter 2005 menu at Horizons. You'll love the spicy, smoky spike that chipotle gives to this sauce. A chipotle is a dried and smoked jalapeno pepper. You can buy them canned in an adobo sauce or dried (just soak the dried chile in hot water for 15 minutes to rehydrate it). There is even chipotle powder now available in some markets. I highly recommend buying the powder if you can find it—it makes a wonderful addition to your spice cabinet. Top this burrito with vegan sour cream and/or any of your favorite Mexican condiments.

Ingredients

4 teaspoons canola oil
1 medium onion, chopped
1 medium red bell pepper, chopped
1 cup vegetable stock
6 plum tomatoes, roughly chopped
1 canned chipotle pepper, chopped, or
   1 teaspoon dried chipotle powder
2 teaspoons sugar
½ teaspoon salt to taste
2 tablespoons Latin Spice blend
16 ounces seitan, drained and rinsed
2 large flour tortillas

Yields

2 servings

Directions

1. In a medium saucepan, heat half the canola oil on medium-high heat until the oil begins to ripple.

2. Add the onion and bell pepper and sauté for 5 minutes.

3. Add the vegetable stock, tomatoes, chipotle, sugar, salt and spice, and simmer for 15 minutes on medium-low heat.

4. Puree mixture with an immersion blender or carefully puree it in a blender.

5. Meanwhile, heat a skillet pan or a wok on high heat with the rest of the canola oil until it begins to ripple.

6. Carefully add the seitan, and brown on each side (about 5 minutes total).

7. Pour the red sauce on the browned seitan and simmer for 5 to 10 minutes or until the sauce does not run anymore and starts caramelizing around the seitan.

8. Heat the tortillas lightly (about 1 minute in a 350-degree oven or about 30 seconds on a gas range burner).

9. Wrap the seitan tightly into each tortilla and serve immediately.

Ingredients

1-pound bag dried black beans
1 or 2 vegetable bouillon cubes
16 ounces seitan, rinsed and drained
1 large onion, chopped
¼ cup chile pepper of your choice,
    chopped (poblano, serrano,
    jalapeno, or habanero)
3 tablespoons Latin Spice blend
2 teaspoons olive oil
2 large collard leaves, center vein
    removed and leaves shredded
1 cup hearts of palm, chopped
2 large orange slices
Salt and pepper to taste

Yields

2 servings

Seitan Feijoada

Feijoada is Brazil's national dish and a vegetarian's nightmare! I have always been intrigued by this concept as I have with all other things Brazilian. So I cleaned up the recipe and replaced all the animal parts with seitan.

The dish is traditionally served with what I have included here (hot peppers, hearts of palm, shredded collards, and orange slices). I would definitely include some fluffy white rice or coconut rice with this dish, and of course, a Caipirinha – Brazil's national drink of cachaça (a sugarcane liquor), lime, and sugar. See you at Carnivale!

Directions

1. Sort through the black beans for debris, such as tiny stones.

2. Rinse the beans and put them in a pot or pressure cooker and cover with at least 3 inches of water. If using a pressure cooker, bring to a boil, then turn off the heat and let them soak for 20 minutes. If cooking the beans in an open pot, let them soak overnight.

   Note: Black beans are the one bean where you want to save the soaking liquid. It's full of flavor and creates that dark black broth that makes black beans so great.

3. Cook the beans in the soaking liquid until they have started to become tender (about 10 to 15 minutes in a pressure cooker or 1 hour or more in an open pot).

4. Add the bouillon, seitan, onions, peppers, and spices, and return to heat to finish cooking (cook open in a pressure cooker).

5. Add more water if the beans start to dry up before the cooking time is finished. Keep at least 1 inches of water above the beans during this time. You will know the beans are done when they are very tender.

6. Stir in the olive oil, and adjust the salt and pepper if necessary.

7. Serve the feijoada in a big bowl and top with the collards, hearts of palm, and orange slices. Garnish with more hot peppers if you wish.

Seitan Feijoada

Ingredients

½ cup dried porcini mushrooms
2 teaspoons canola oil
1 cup onion, chopped
4 cloves garlic, crushed
¼ cup white wine
16 ounces of seitan, rinsed, drained, and finely chopped or coarsely pureed in a food processor
12 plum tomatoes, coarsely chopped
½ cup vegetable stock
1 teaspoon dried oregano
1½ teaspoons salt
1 teaspoon black pepper
1 teaspoon dried rosemary
1 teaspoon dried sage
1 pound cooked pasta of your choice
1 tablespoon extra virgin olive oil

Yields

2 to 3 servings

Pasta with Ground Seitan & Porcini Mushroom Sauce

When I was little, my parents had hired this Italian carpenter who was building them some furniture for the house. One day, they drove us up to his house in the country to check on some of the pieces. I'll never forget the ride. Down a long gravel driveway lined with sycamore trees and across a bridge straddling a little stream, there was his house in the distance, all wood and stone. He had built it himself. I always think back to that property when I envision a peaceful country home to settle down in one day. It was that perfect. But even more so, that day sparked one of my earliest and most vivid food memories. We were walking through this guy's house when we stopped in the kitchen, where his wife was making a fresh tomato sauce that smelled like the most heavenly thing you could possibly imagine eating. The aromas are still so vivid to me.

When I got older, I grew my own tomatoes in my parents backyard and tried to duplicate that sauce. Even now as a chef, I still make fresh tomato sauce for dinner in honor of that great memory.

So I had high hopes for my first trip to Italy. I imagined that this sauce, this smell would be everywhere, wafting from peoples homes and from little cafes. It was winter on the Amalfi coast and, although the lemon trees were filled with football sized fruit, I didn't experience the fresh, light cuisine that I had envisioned. Instead, it was pasta, pasta, and more pasta! No complaints, I absolutely love pasta, and we'll go deep into Italy for this wintery, meaty dish of stewed seitan and porcini mushrooms.

Porcini mushrooms are a product that actually dries really well, concentrating their already deep flavor. They rehydrate beautifully, and the water they soak in during rehydration makes a wonderful cooking liquid to add to stocks. This recipe is just as good without the seitan, and although any pasta would be great under this sauce, my choice would be good old-fashioned spaghetti.

Directions

1. Place the dried porcini mushrooms in 2 cups water, bring to a boil, and let stand for 10 to 15 minutes.

2. Strain the mushrooms and reserve the liquid.

3. In a large saucepot, heat the canola oil over medium-high heat until rippling.

4. Add the onion and garlic and brown lightly for about 3 to 5 minutes.

5. Add the wine and simmer, allowing it to reduce for 1 minute.

6. Add all the other ingredients, including the soaking liquid from the porcini mushrooms, but excluding the extra virgin olive oil and the pasta.

7. Cover and simmer on very low heat for 20 to 30 minutes, stirring occasionally.

8. You can add the precooked pasta right into the sauce at this point, or just pour the sauce over it.

9. Drizzle with the extra virgin olive oil just before serving.

Pan-Seared Tofu with Tortilla Crust & Tomato-Tortilla Sauce

Pan-Seared Tofu with Tortilla Crust & Tomato-Tortilla Sauce

Tortillas are one of the great foods of the galaxy, and we will celebrate corn tortilla chips as the main theme of this Mexican tofu dish. The crushed tortillas give texture to the encrusted tofu, and the tortillas cooked into the sauce add a great dimension of flavor while serving as a thickener. This dish is great with rice, avocado, and a simple salad of cilantro leaves, lettuce, and lime.

Directions

1. In a saucepan or sauté pan, heat the ½ tablespoon of oil for the sauce over medium-high heat until it is gently rippling.

2. Add the onion and garlic and brown lightly for about 3 to 5 minutes.

3. Next add the tomatoes, spice blend, ½ cup of tortillas, vegetable stock, salt, pepper, and cumin (as well as the chipotles and/or jalapenos if you choose to use them).

4. Let the sauce simmer on medium for 5 minutes, then remove from heat.

5. Let the sauce cool slightly, then puree in a blender.

6. Pan-sear the tofu as shown on page 15 of the *In Your Kitchen* section.

7. When done, remove tofu from the pan and, in a mixing bowl, toss with the crushed tortilla crumbs.

8. Serve with the sauce beneath the tofu and sprinkle extra crumbs on top of the tofu if the mixture isn't sticking well enough.

Sauce Ingredients

1½ tablespoons canola oil
½ cup onion, chopped
1 clove garlic, crushed
6 plum tomatoes, roughly chopped
2 teaspoons Latin Spice blend
½ cup tortilla chips or soft corn tortillas (crushed or torn)
2 cups vegetable stock
½ teaspoon salt
½ teaspoon pepper
½ teaspoon ground or whole cumin
1 chipotle (optional)
1 jalapeno (optional)

Tofu Ingredients

1 (16-ounce) block of tofu, cut into 3 equal slabs
Tofu Spice blend for coating tofu (see page 15)
A few tablespoons or canola or olive oil for searing the tofu
2 cups tortilla chips, crushed in a food processor

Yields

2 to 3 servings

Sauce Ingredients

2 tablespoons margarine
¼ cup vegan mayo
1 teaspoon Dijon mustard
Salt and pepper to taste
1 teaspoon fresh tarragon, chopped
(thyme or dill will change the flavor,
but make fine substitutes)

Tofu Ingredients

3 English muffins
Margarine for spreading (optional)
1 (16-ounce) block of tofu, cut into
3 equal slabs
Tofu Spice blend for coating tofu
(see page 15)
A few tablespoons of canola oil for
searing the tofu
1 tablespoon canola oil for frying bacon
6 slices vegetarian bacon
1 very large ripe beefsteak or slicing
tomato, cut into 3 thick slices

Yields

3 servings

Tofu Benedict with Vegan Béarnaise

Brunch is always a wild occasion at Horizons. To be here first thing on a Sunday morning throws everyone off, but in my mind, that adds to the magic. I love brunch at Horizons. It gives me the chance to do things we never do for dinner—like this Tofu Benedict. It's been on every brunch menu we've done, in one version or another.

This dish works well as an in-home celebration dish for a Saturday or Sunday morning. Wake up early one morning when the sun is shining through the window, go for a walk, get a few chores done, and then treat yourself and some family or friends to this cleaned-up classic—sans the heart attack. For variations, try cooking some fresh spinach and using that as a layer beneath the tofu. A pinch of cayenne in the sauce is a trick you can use to wake up anyone who doesn't want coffee! And for a Caribbean touch, some sautéed, ripe plantains give it a whole new dimension.

Directions

1. Bring the margarine to room temperature, letting it soften to the point that it is more melted than solid.

2. In a mixing bowl, gently whisk together the softened margarine with the other sauce ingredients.

   Note: If the sauce is too thick, drizzle in about 2 teaspoons cold water to thin it. If it breaks and liquefies, then refrigerate it immediately to thicken again.

3. Toast the English muffins and spread on some additional margarine if desired.

4. Pan-sear the tofu as shown on page 15 of the *In Your Kitchen* section.

5. In a separate sauté pan, heat the remaining 1 tablespoon of canola oil over medium-high heat until it is gently rippling.

6. Lightly fry the vegetarian bacon for about 45 seconds on each side.

   Note: Do not overcook the bacon or it will get tough!

7. Layer the dish, starting with the muffin, bacon, tofu, and tomato.

8. Drizzle the béarnaise sauce on top and serve immediately.

Tofu Benedict with Vegan Béarnaise

Ingredients

16 ounce seitan, drained and rinsed
1 tablespoon capers
1 cup white onion, chopped
1 cup green bell pepper, chopped
½ cup ketchup
¼ cup flour
2 tablespoons olive oil
2 tablespoons green olives, pitted
¼ cup raisins
4 tablespoons Latin Spice blend
16 ounces veggie burgers or
   vegetarian ground beef

Yields

4 to 6 servings

Cuban Seitan Meatloaf Picadillo

If there were a road to Cuba from Key West, you could drive there in an hour and a half! It's amazing how close Cuba really is, yet how far away it seems. There will be a time in the future when we will reconnect with this seemingly distant world. Until then, we have Miami!

Next time that you are in Miami, check out Calle Ocho (8th Street) and the Cuban community that exists there. You can get an authentic taste of these two worlds coming together.

I love the concept of picadillo, which is a meat stew with olives, raisins and capers in a tomato-based sauce. I have brought these flavors into this meatloaf recipe. Check out the way the salty taste plays against the sweetness. This is a large recipe but it freezes well.

Directions

1. Preheat oven to 350 degrees.

2. Puree all ingredients in a food processor until it reaches a chunky paste.

3. Place in a lightly oiled loaf pan covered with foil and bake for 25 to 30 minutes.

   Note: You can also form this mix into meatballs or burgers. Bake for 10 to 12 minutes at 450 degrees.

4. Serve with mashed potatoes or rice and your favorite tomato sauce.

Suggested Variation

If you prefer a stew version to the meatloaf version, do not use the food processor. In addition, simply omit the flour and simmer all ingredients in a large pot with 1½ cups vegetable stock and 4 chopped plum tomatoes for about 25 minutes. The stew is fantastic served over rice.

YOUR VEGGIE BBQ

It's happened to all of us. Your friends or family were kind enough to buy you veggie dogs for the big BBQ they're having. You arrive and grab your paper plate, and there's your veggie dog on the grill, rolling around with the mystery-meat dogs. After the BBQ master makes fun of your veggie dog and asks, "What's in them, anyway?" (like someone who eats real hot dogs should be asking that...). He then goes on to say, "I think this one is yours…" and puts the dog in your whole wheat hippie bun. It's happened to all of us: the ridicule, the looks, the questions. Where's the reward? Your veggie dog is dried out and cooked to a crispy cracker. Well, here are some tips to a very successful veggie BBQ:

1. Remember that most mock-meat products these days contain very little or no fat at all. Brush a little oil on them to prevent them from sticking and to give them a nice appealing shine.

2. You don't have to worry about salmonella. You don't have to cook it through. Most soy products literally take only 2 to 3 minutes on medium-high heat to be ready.

3. Don't use heavy, sticky sauces too early. The sugars in them will burn and create a goopy mess on the grates. Brush BBQ and teriyaki-type sauces on during the last minute of cooking, and don't turn them too much.

4. When you first put something on the grill, leave it alone. I know you are anxious to flip something. You have your hat and apron on, and your giant spatula is ready in hand. Leave it alone for the first 2 minutes. If you try to turn it too early, it will stick, fall apart, and make a mess. Let the grill do its work and wait for those char marks!

5. For a special rustic touch, get cans of baked beans and sauerkraut. Peel the label, open the top, and put the can right on the grill, early.

6. Vegetables, like corn and portobella mushrooms, grill very easily whole. Peppers and onions should be left in large chunks (not thin slices that can burn or fall through the grates). Zucchini and eggplant can be sliced into planks and are amazing on the grill.

7. Don't be afraid of winter grilling. Some of my fondest food memories are grilling in the cold weather and even in a snowstorm (a little brandy and hot chocolate helps a lot). It's a great way to bring the outdoors in during the winter. ■

SIDES

Ingredients

2 teaspoons salt
1 teaspoon black pepper
¼ cup canola oil
2 heads cauliflower, chopped into
   large chunks
¼ cup garlic, chopped
1 bunch parsley (flat or curly),
   finely chopped
2 tablespoons white wine
2 tablespoons extra virgin olive oil
2 tablespoons margarine
½ cup plum tomatoes, chopped
   (optional)

Yields

6 servings

Caramelized Cauliflower in Spanish Green Garlic Sauce

Don't mistake Spanish food for Latin-American food. True, there are Spanish roots all over the Americas, but back in Spain, you will never see an enchilada or burrito. They do love their garlic, though, and that's why I love them.

You also rarely see cilantro in traditional Spanish cooking. Again, that's more of a Latin-American ingredient. The green herb that dominates classic Spanish cuisine is parsley, especially in this Basque-inspired sauce. Using parsley for flavor rather than garnish really highlights the diversity of this underrated herb.

Directions

1. Preheat oven to 450 degrees.

2. In a large mixing bowl, combine the salt, pepper and canola oil, then toss in the cauliflower.

3. Spread out the coated cauliflower on a large baking tray.

4. Roast the cauliflower for 15 to 20 minutes or until the edges start to curl and brown.

5. Remove the roasted cauliflower from the oven and return it to the mixing bowl.

6. Toss the remaining ingredients with the roasted cauliflower.

Caramelized Cauliflower in Spanish Green Garlic Sauce (without tomatoes)

Ingredients

6 ounces (½ bag) frozen edamame
   beans, shelled
1 garlic clove
½ cup olive oil
6 large Yukon gold or all-purpose
   potatoes, peel off as much skin as
   you like
½ to 1 cup water (reserved from
   cooking the potatoes)
1 teaspoon salt
1 teaspoon pepper

Yields

4 servings

Edamame Mashed Potatoes

This decadent starch harmonizes beautifully with the Korean Grilled Tofu (recipe on page 109). For extra amazing touches, try a drizzle of white truffle oil!

Directions

1. Begin by heating two pots of water on the stove—one for the edamame and a larger one for the potatoes.

2. Boil the edamame with the garlic clove for 3 to 5 minutes, then drain the water.

3. Let edamame cool slightly, then puree it in a food processor, adding ¼ cup of the oil and just enough water to make a thick paste.

4. Roughly chop the potatoes and add enough water to cover them.

5. Boil potatoes about 15 minutes or until tender.

6. When the potatoes are done, drain the water (saving about 1 cup of the cooking water for mashing).

7. Mash the potatoes with the edamame puree, salt, pepper, and the remaining ¼ cup of oil.

8. As necessary, add enough of the reserved cooking water to bring the mashed potatoes to the desired consistency.

Note: A proper potato masher gives the best results.

Coconut & Red Chile Broccoli

There is just something so incredible about red chile paste and coconut milk together. It's a mind-blowing combination of flavors. In between the heat of the chiles and the luxurious creaminess of the coconut milk rests the flavors of the curry paste. Curry paste is a wet spice mixture available in small cans at Asian markets. Make sure to read the ingredients as some contain shrimp! The three main colors of chile paste available vary from red to yellow to green. My favorite is the green as it's heavy on kaffir lime and lemon grass. The yellow is a more aromatic blend, usually featuring cinnamon, cardamom, and star anise. The red is a fiery chile-based blend. They are all wonderfully powerful and pack an intense amount of flavor.

Directions

1. In a food processor or in a mixing bowl with whisk, combine all of the ingredients except the broccoli and set aide.

2. Cook the broccoli as you like: steamed, sautéed, or stir-fried.

3. Transfer the hot broccoli into a mixing bowl and toss with the sauce.

4. Garnish with any or all of the recommended greens.

Ingredients

4 to 6 cups fresh broccoli, stems trimmed
1 cup coconut milk
2 teaspoons curry paste (red, yellow, or green)
1 teaspoon sugar
½ teaspoon salt
1 teaspoon Sriracha or Sambal Olek chile paste (more if you like)
Fresh mint, scallions, cilantro, or basil (for garnishes)

Yields

2 to 4 servings

Truffled Golden Beet Slaw (without cabbage and carrots)

Truffled Golden Beet Slaw

I made a version of this beautifully fresh, crunchy, raw slaw for some of our favorite customers for Passover one year. It was so good that I couldn't stop eating it. It's so easy and makes a great salad, side, or condiment on your favorite sandwich.

Directions

1. Put the beets, cabbage, and carrots through the shredder blade of a food processor and place in a large mixing bowl.

2. In a small bowl, combine the dressing ingredients.

3. Drizzle the dressing over the shredded vegetables and toss to combine.

4. Cover and chill for at least 30 minutes before serving.

Slaw Ingredients

1 large golden beet, peeled
½ head green cabbage, outer leaves removed and cut into small chunks (in order for it to go in the food processor chute)
1 carrot, peeled

Dressing Ingredients

1 bunch scallions, finely chopped
2½ tablespoons white truffle oil
2 tablespoons fresh lemon juice
2 tablespoons olive oil
1 teaspoon sherry vinegar
1 teaspoon fresh chopped dill
1 teaspoon salt
1 teaspoon pepper

Yields

2 to 4 servings

Ingredients

2 cups quinoa, cooked
1 tablespoon olive oil
¼ cup onion, finely diced
2 cloves garlic, crushed
6 plum tomatoes, diced
¼ cup vegetable stock (more to
    moisten if necessary)
1 teaspoon smoked paprika
1 teaspoon chipotle puree or powder
1 teaspoon salt
1 teaspoon pepper

Yields

4 to 6 servings

Smoked Chile & Tomato Quinoa

An ancient Aztec food and Peruvian staple, quinoa is the world's oldest grain and quite possibly the most interesting and nutritious. I love its delicate, couscous-like qualities, yet I'm impressed by how well it can handle powerful sauces like this one.

Directions

1. Soak the quinoa in warm water for about 20 minutes, and then drain and rinse thoroughly through a fine mesh strainer.

2. Cook quinoa according to package directions.

3. Once the water has been absorbed, remove from heat and spread out the cooked quinoa on a sheet pan to cool.

4. Meanwhile, heat the olive oil in a large sauté pan.

5. Add the onions and garlic, and sauté 1 to 3 minutes or until they are toasty and translucent.

6. Add the tomatoes and sauté for 3 to 5 minutes or until the tomatoes start to break down.

7. Add the vegetable stock, and simmer on medium-low heat until the tomatoes have really loosened up and started to become a sauce.

8. Add the paprika, chipotle, salt, and pepper, and stir to combine.

9. Fold in the quinoa and serve.

Tofu "Crab" Mashed Potatoes

There's nothing like sitting at an outdoor café with the ocean in view or relaxing on a pier with a deck bar and boaters pulling up for lunch, like Lorelei's in Islamorada in the Florida Keys or Pusser's waterfront bar in Annapolis, Maryland.

Usually everyone there is eating seafood. If you're feeling left out, then try this dish. The "crab" also goes wonderfully well over spaghetti for an entrée—one of my favorites!

Mashed Potato Ingredients

3 large Yukon Gold or all-purpose potatoes
1 tablespoon margarine
½ teaspoon salt
½ teaspoon pepper

Tofu "Crab" Ingredients

8 ounces (½ block) tofu, cut into very small dice
¼ cup onion, cut into very small dice
¼ cup green bell pepper, cut in a very small dice
½ tablespoon garlic, crushed
2 tablespoons plum tomato, diced (save any juices)
2 tablespoons white wine
1½ tablespoons seafood seasoning
3 tablespoons canola oil

Yields

4 to 6 servings

Directions

1. Preheat oven to 450 degrees.

2. Begin by heating a large pot to boil the potatoes.

3. Roughly chop the potatoes and add enough water to cover them.

4. Boil potatoes about 15 minutes or until tender.

5. Meanwhile, toss all the "crab" ingredients in a large mixing bowl.

6. Spread out the crab mixture on a roasting tray and bake for 10 minutes or until the top becomes golden brown and then set aside.

7. When the potatoes are done, drain the water (saving about 1 cup of the cooking water for mashing).

8. Mash the potatoes with the margarine, salt, and pepper.

9. As necessary, add enough of the reserved cooking water to bring the mashed potatoes to the desired consistency.

   Note: A proper potato masher gives the best results.

10. Combine the "crab" mixture with the potatoes.

Suggested Variation

If making this a pasta dish, double the white wine, garlic, and tomatoes. Add ¼ cup margarine and ½ cup vegetable stock for 1 pound of pasta.

Ingredients

2 cups traditional couscous
2 cups boiling water
1 teaspoon preserved lemon, finely
   chopped
½ cup onion, finely chopped
½ teaspoon ground cumin
1 pinch ground coriander
1 pinch ground clove
Salt and pepper to taste
2 tablespoons olive oil
¼ cup fresh mint leaves, chopped
½ cup almonds, slivered or crushed
¼ cup oil-cured black olives, pitted
   and chopped
1 tablespoon fresh lemon juice

Yields

4 to 6 servings

Couscous with Preserved Lemon, Almonds & Moroccan Olives

Traditional couscous is so easy to make. Simply place it in a mixing bowl and pour boiling water over it, and it cooks itself. This is a nice side dish for grilled or roasted vegetables or tofu-kabobs. The North African accents in this recipe add a nice exotic note, while not overpowering the taste or texture of the couscous itself.

Directions

1. Have a pot of boiling water ready on the stove (you'll need about 2 cups or more if the couscous becomes too dry).

2. Meanwhile, in a large mixing bowl, add the dry couscous, preserved lemon, onion, cumin, coriander, clove, salt and pepper.

3. Pour the boiling water over the couscous and let stand for about 5 minutes.

4. Fluff with a fork, making sure the couscous is cooked and moist (add water if it isn't quite there yet).

5. Mix in the olive oil, mint, almonds, olives, and lemon juice, stirring thoroughly to combine.

Couscous with Preserved Lemon, Almonds & Moroccan Olives

Ingredients

1 large celery root, peeled and
    julienned finely by hand or on a
    mandoline (should produce 2 cups)
½ cup vegan mayo
1 tablespoon Dijon mustard
1 teaspoon lemon juice
½ teaspoon salt
½ teaspoon pepper
1 tablespoon olive oil
2 teaspoons capers, chopped
2 teaspoons cornichons, chopped
    (French baby pickles)
2 teaspoons red onion, finely chopped

Yields

2 to 4 servings

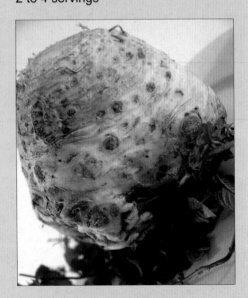

Celery Root Rémoulade

Where do chefs take their honeymoon? The south of France, of course. From the beautiful Cote De Azure in Nice, Kate and I ventured south to the French island of Corsica. One day we were taking a picnic lunch to the beach, and I bought a celery root (AKA celeriac) salad in the local market. It was unlike any celery root I have ever prepared or tasted. Perfectly blanched and dressed in an incredible tangy and creamy mustard sauce. Years later on the Caribbean French island of St. Martin, I found it again in a small market, it tasted exactly as I had remembered—perfectly creamy, tangy, complex, and absolutely addictive.

Celeriac is a knobby, alien-looking plant root from which we get celery seeds. It's a close relative to the more familiar stalk celery. It has a beautiful starchy texture with hints of celery and parsnip. CAUTION: Be very careful since the celery root is a very hard and awkward vegetable with which to work.

Directions

1. Bring a medium saucepot of water to a boil, and have a bowl of ice water ready.

2. Once the water boils, drop in the celery root and blanch for 1 minute, then remove it and shock in the ice water.

3. When the celery root has cooled in the water, drain the water and set the celery root aside.

4. In a medium mixing bowl, thoroughly combine the rest of the ingredients; adjust the salt and pepper to taste.

5. Make sure the celery root is well-drained, and add it to the dressing, tossing thoroughly to coat.

6. Cover and chill the dressed celery root in the refrigerator for about 20 to 30 minutes.

Suggested Variation

The celery root rémoulade makes a great sandwich topping in place of coleslaw. It also can be served atop red tomato slices for a lunch appetizer and as a great antipasto component with roasted peppers, olives, and marinated mushrooms. Or, it's great on its own.

Garlic Green Beans with Marcona Almonds & Vegan Tarragon Butter

Spanish Marcona almonds are unlike any almond you have ever tasted. They are unique, but frightfully expensive, so feel free to use conventional almonds if you don't want to splurge.

Directions

1. In a large skillet, heat the oil on medium heat until it ripples.

2. Add the garlic and immediately put the string beans on top.

3. When the garlic starts to brown (after 1 to 2 minutes), add the water and cover the pot.

4. Steam the beans until the desired tenderness—some people like their green beans crunchy, while some prefer theirs a bit more tender.

5. When done to your liking, transfer the beans to a mixing bowl, and add the margarine, tarragon, salt and pepper.

6. Toss until the margarine melts, and then garnish with the almonds.

Ingredients

1 tablespoon olive oil
2 tablespoons garlic, chopped
1 pound French beans or green beans, ends trimmed
1 cup water
2 tablespoons margarine, softened
2 teaspoons fresh tarragon, chopped
Salt and pepper to taste
¼ cup Spanish Marcona almonds, chopped or crushed

Yields

4 to 6 servings

Ingredients

3 medium zucchini
2 cups plum tomatoes, finely diced
    and tossed with 1 teaspoon salt
1½ tablespoons extra virgin olive oil
½ teaspoon black pepper
1 cup fresh basil leaves, chopped
1 tablespoon fresh lemon juice
½ cup crushed cauliflower (grated or
    pulsed in a food processor)

Yields

2 to 4 servings

Raw Zucchini Fettuccine

I love raw vegetable dishes and this is one of my all-time favorites. You will need a mandolin for this recipe, so please be very careful! The secret to this recipe is the "tomato water." It is the juice released from the tomatoes once they are diced and salted. Make sure to cut the (very ripe) tomatoes into very small dice or the trick won't work. The fresh basil gives a great summer accent and the crumbled cauliflower on top suggests the addition of a tasty Parmesan.

Directions

1. Shave the zucchini on a mandolin using only the wider vertical cutting blade on the outer part of the zucchini (not the seeds). You should be able to get 4 to 6 cuts on each side before hitting the seeds.

   Note: The zucchini should be very thin, but not paper thin. It should also be thick enough to pick up and toss with the sauce in a bowl without breaking. You may use the fine vertical blade for "angel hair," or just use the main cutter blade (and not the vertical blades) to get wide sheets of pappardelle "noodles."

2. Drain some of the tomato water from the salted tomatoes, using about half of the tomato water and the lemon juice to mix in with the cauliflower.

3. Toss the zucchini with all the other ingredients, including the rest of the tomato water.

4. Cover and chill the zucchini fettuccine in the refrigerator for about 20 to 30 minutes or until the zucchini softens.

5. Mound the zucchini up in bowls and top with the crumbled cauliflower.

Raw Zucchini Fettuccine (without cauliflower topping)

Ingredients

1 pound snow peas, ends trimmed
1 tablespoon mild white miso paste
2 teaspoons tamari soy sauce
2 teaspoons sesame oil
1 teaspoon rice wine vinegar
¼ cups scallions, roughly chopped
1 small garlic clove
¼ cup water
1 teaspoon canola or peanut oil
¼ teaspoon black pepper

Yields

4 to 6 servings

Snow Peas with Miso Vinaigrette

Fresh, bright, green, and crunchy, snow peas pair so easily with Asian ingredients. This flavorful vinaigrette can also be used on a simple leaf salad as well as a marinade for grilled or baked tofu.

Directions

1. Blend all ingredients except the snow peas in a food processor.

2. Lightly steam, boil, or sauté the snow peas until they just turn bright green.

3. Toss the warm peas in the dressing.

4. Cover and chill immediately for at least 30 minutes before serving.

MORGAN'S ROCK

RIVAS - SAN JUAN DEL SUR - GRANADA—I watch the signs of the towns, and then the towns themselves pass by my window. We are in Nicaragua and on our way to the Pacific coast. Part of me is tempted to ask the driver to pull over at the little bars and restaurants that we see. I would love nothing better than to sit down and support the local economy. "*Hola, yo soy vegetariano. No como carne ni pollo ni pescado.*" I can imagine the looks on their faces. Nicaraguan cuisine is overwhelmingly meat-based, but I know that with a creative cook, anything is possible.

The ride from Managua to the Pacific where we are staying is some 2½ hours. We pass many small towns, some best seen from the rearview mirror, while others are so colorfully inviting. In my experience with Central American people, I find that they are among the friendliest that I have had the pleasure to meet.

Mention Nicaragua and many Americans envision the lingering dust of an utterly embarrassing American "covert" operation in the 80s. That, along with a colorful history of rebels, dictators, natural disasters, and crooks has prevented Nicaragua from reaping the benefits of Eco-tourism that have reshaped Costa Rica in recent years. As this shift occurs on the Pacific coast, Kate and I are fortunate to have seen some of this beautiful country before it gets too built up.

There was a time in my life when I would have lumped all Central American food together. Although many of their basic ingredients are similar, the different cuisines of Central American countries are surprisingly unique. Nicaragua's cuisine may just be the best.

We arrive at our hotel, Morgan's Rock Hacienda, which is a cluster of comfortable cabanas built on a hillside overlooking the ocean. The place is small and rustic, but filled with so many comforts. Luckily the food was so superb that we forgot the little bars and restaurants that we saw on the way. Gallo pinto is the Nicaraguan version of rice and beans, traditionally vegetarian and delicious. Tejadas are long, fried plantain strips, sweet and crisp-perfect for dipping. The corn tortillas are thick, unlike any Mexican version I have known, somewhere between a Mexican corn tortilla, an arepa, and a pita, and they are absolutely addictive. Cebollita is an onion and chile-based relish, kind of like a tomato-less salsa that compliments beans beautifully. Many of the vegetables that we ate came from the hotel's organic farm. We enjoyed beautiful salad greens and incredible chilled soups like cucumber yogurt and roasted sweet chile.

Dinners are served by romantic candlelight, with the sounds of the waves crashing in the distance. Our cold glasses of Flor de Cana rum sweat beads of condensation in the soft tropical night air. I'm just a sucker for scenes like that.

I think of what might have been in this land. And by that, I am referring to the fact that the Panama Canal was originally supposed to be built in Nicaragua. Plans were drawn, surveys conducted, and all was set to go. Last-minute political agendas and secret handshakes diverted the project to Panama.

I have seen the Panama Canal. I have seen the biggest ships you could possibly imagine glide poetically through the rivers and lakes. What cannot be understated is what the canal has done for the Panamanians. The United States built the canal with the understanding that they would operate it for the first 100 years, then it would be owned by Panama. When I visited around the turn of the century, Panama seemed already quite better off than any of its neighbors. As I watched a giant cargo ship from Mitsubishi float by, I asked the taxi driver how much it costs to use the canal. He indicated $50,000 for that Mitsubishi freighter, loaded with cars bound for United States showrooms. That's a lot of dough, yet still cheaper than sailing around Africa or safer than going around Cape Horn.

The next day, we are splashing in the ocean. The warm wavy water is impossible to leave. It's just too much fun. Kate eventually goes back to the beach to relax, and I indulge in one of my favorite passions—floating in the ocean, imagining what my menu would look like if Horizons were here on this beach. Well, I'd serve grilled tofu with island spices over one of those incredible tortillas with cebollita and avocado; tamarind and rum-glazed seitan over curried rice; and native vegetable and bean stew with coconut milk, chiles, cilantro and tejadas. Okay, now I'm really hungry. Lunchtime! ■

Ingredients

1 cup peanut butter
1½ cups soy milk
¼ cup sugar
½ teaspoon salt
3 cups chocolate chips
1 cup corn cereal (flakes or puffs)

Yields

1 dozen bombs

Restaurant action with bombs in the making!

Chocolate Peanut Butter Bombs

Ever since I put them on the menu, my Chocolate Peanut Butter Bombs have developed a cult-like following. I struggled for a while, keeping them on the menu, then taking them off. On one hand, they are a chocolate lover's dream—rich, dark, soft chocolate with just the right amount of creamy peanut butter to make the bitter chocolate even more delectably rich. On the other hand, they are very small and simple, and I always feel like I should be serving a more complicated chocolate dessert at the restaurant.

So here's a simple recipe for all the die-hard "Bomb" fans—this one's for you! Just be sure to use the best quality chocolate and peanut butter you can find.

Directions

1. In a food processor, combine the peanut butter, ½ cup of the soy milk, sugar, and salt, and mix until smooth.

2. Using a microwave or double-boiler, melt the chocolate chips with 1 cup of the soy milk. Whisk thoroughly to make sure chocolate is well melted and perfectly smooth.

3. Transfer the warm chocolate to a squeeze bottle.

4. Line a muffin tin or cupcake molds with paper muffin liners.

5. Squeeze about 2 tablespoons of the warm chocolate into each paper muffin liner.

6. Scoop about 2 tablespoons of the peanut butter cream into the center of the chocolate on the bottom of the muffin liner.

7. Squeeze the rest of the warm chocolate into the muffin liners, to cover the peanut butter cream.

8. Refrigerate bombs for at least 1 hour before serving.

9. Meanwhile, grind cereal to a fine powder in the food processor and store in an airtight container.

10. When ready to serve, remove paper liner and toss the bomb in the cereal crumbs.

11. At the restaurant, we serve the bomb on top of a round piece of brownie with a scoop of home-made peanut butter ice cream.

Toasted Coconut Chocolate Mousse

During our first trip to Nicaragua, Rich and I stayed on a hacienda called Morgan's Rock. Absolutely everything was made on the hacienda. While we were impressed with everything we ate on that trip, the chocolate mousse was a highlight. They weren't very modest about it either, which was a good thing. That way, every guest got to enjoy it.

My version aims to be just as rich and decadent in the chocolate department, but I use coconut to add additional flavor as well as nice textural contrast by coating the mousse in the toasted coconut flakes.

Ingredients

1 cup flour
½ teaspoon baking powder
¼ cup cocoa powder
Pinch salt
4 cups chocolate chips
1 (13-ounce) can coconut milk
1½ tablespoons margarine
8 ounces silken tofu
½ cup shredded coconut flakes, unsweetened

Yields
6 servings

Directions

1. In a large mixing bowl, combine the flour, baking powder, cocoa powder and salt.

2. Using a microwave or double-boiler, melt the chocolate chips with the coconut milk and margarine.

3. In a blender, combine the melted chocolate mixture with the silken tofu until smooth.

4. Add half the blended chocolate mixture to the flour mixture and stir until totally smooth.

5. Add the remaining chocolate to flour mixture and stir again.

6. Pour immediately into a casserole dish or deep bowl to set.

7. Place in the refrigerator and allow to cool for at least 2 hours.

8. Meanwhile, heat the coconut flakes in a sauté pan on medium heat, stirring occasionally to toast evenly.

9. Remove coconut from heat and allow to cool in a small bowl.

10. When mousse is set, use an ice cream scoop to form small balls of the chilled mousse, and toss them in the coconut flakes just before serving.

Tahitian Vanilla Crème Brûlée

Tahitian Vanilla Crème Brûlée

When I first assumed the role of Pastry Chef at Horizons, I vowed to myself that I would not try to recreate classic dairy desserts like cheesecake, ice cream, or crème brûlée. I figured instead that my focus would be on fruit, not wanting to compete with the richness of dairy desserts unless I could really nail the recipes and make desserts that would impress the most committed dairy-eaters. After lots of trial and error, I finally developed a few recipes that I approved, and I have been baking cheesecakes and serving crème brûlée ever since. No one was interested in chilled fruit soups or fancy fruit tarts; they wanted vegan cheesecake! So here is one of these recipes I'm willing to divulge. The cheesecake recipe is still a secret!

Ingredients

4 (13-ounce) cans coconut milk
½ vanilla bean
1 tablespoon vanilla extract
Dash salt
1 tablespoon agar
½ cup agave syrup
About ¼ cup white cane sugar
½ pineapple, chopped (for garnish)

Yields

8 servings

Directions

1. In a medium saucepan over medium heat, combine all ingredients, except the cane sugar and pineapple.

2. Bring mixture to a boil, then allow to simmer for about 15 minutes, until agar is fully dissolved.

3. Remove the vanilla bean, and transfer the mixture to a blender.

4. Slice the vanilla bean lengthwise and scrap a knife's edge along the inside to remove the seeds.

5. Add the seeds to the mixture in the blender and blend for about 1 minute to ensure that all the agar is completely dissolved.

6. Pour blended mixture into 8 crème brûlée dishes or other ovenware.

7. Cool in the refrigerator for at least 2 hours before serving.

8. When ready to serve, sprinkle each custard with a fine layer of the cane sugar, then "burn" carefully using a blow torch.

   Note: Cane sugar, rather than fructose or other granular sweeteners, achieves the best crackly crust for the custard.

9. Garnish with fresh pineapple on top or however you like (coconut whipped cream, cookies, etc.).

Ingredients for Brownies

3 cups flour
2 cups sugar
1½ teaspoons baking powder
2¾ cups chocolate chips
½ cup shortening
½ cup margarine
2 tablespoons instant coffee
2 cups soy milk

Ingredients for Icing

3 cups powdered sugar
¼ cup margarine, softened
1 teaspoon vanilla extract
¼ cup cold coffee or espresso

Yields

12 big brownies

Espresso Brownies

My first memories of coffee date back to when I was 8 years old and worked part time at my mom's office. On the way to work each morning, we'd stop at the local bakery, and I was treated to a mini cup of coffee with lots of milk and sugar, as well as the most delicious chocolate brownie you could ever imagine. It was so dark and fudgy. There were chocolate chips in the actual brownie, and decadent icing on top. No wonder I was a superfast filing assistant! In any case, I still dream of that morning combination, and to this day, I don't think that brownies are complete without some frosting.

Directions

1. Preheat oven to 350 degrees.

2. Line a half-sheet pan with parchment paper (or coat it with margarine and a light dusting of flour).

3. In a large mixing bowl, combine the flour, sugar, and baking powder.

4. In a medium size saucepan, melt the chocolate chips with the shortening, margarine, instant coffee, and milk over very low heat, stirring with a spoon until very smooth.

5. Remove chocolate from heat and allow to cool for a few minutes.

6. Add the melted ingredients to the dry ingredients, and stir quickly until combined.

7. Pour the batter into the sheet pan, and bake for 30 minutes, turning halfway through to ensure even baking.

8. Meanwhile, make the icing by combining all icing ingredients in a food processor.

9. Allow the brownie to cool thoroughly (about 1½ hours) before icing.

10. Garnish with cocoa powder, powdered sugar, coffee beans, or melted chocolate.

Espresso Brownies

Bittersweet Chocolate Tart

Bittersweet Chocolate Tart

This is a very simple dessert that serves as a great base for all kinds of imaginative sauces and ice creams. I've served it with peanut butter ice cream and smoked agave-tequila sauce, red hot cinnamon ice cream and candied almonds, pistachio ice cream and balsamic strawberries. No matter how you serve it, the tart makes a dramatic presentation for any chocolate lover. Be sure to use the best quality chocolate chips.

Directions

1. In a food processor, combine flour, cornstarch, salt, margarine, and shortening. While mixing, add the oil and half the water.

2. Stop the food processor and feel the dough (see *Working with Crusts* below for the desired consistency). Add more water if necessary.

3. Remove the dough from the food processor and roll it out on a floured surface.

4. Transfer the dough to a 10-inch, fluted pie pan. Cover and chill the crust in the refrigerator for about 10 minutes.

5. Preheat oven to 375 degrees.

6. After the crust has cooled, place it in the oven and bake for 12 to 15 minutes or until golden brown.

7. Remove crust from oven then allow to cool.

8. In a medium saucepan over very low heat, combine the chocolate chips and 2 cups of the soy milk, stirring occasionally until smooth.

9. In a small mixing bowl, create a roux by adding the remaining soy milk, salt, and flour, combining well and leaving no lumps.

10. When the chocolate chips have melted, add the soy milk mixture and increase the heat to medium.

11. Bring to a near-boil to activate the roux, while being careful to keep the chocolate from burning.

12. Pour the chocolate into the cooling pie shell and allow to cool to room temperature for at least 30 minutes, then refrigerate for at least 2 hours before serving. Store the tart in an airtight container in the refrigerator.

13. Garnish and serve as desired.

Crust Ingredients

1½ cups flour
1 tablespoon cornstarch
Pinch salt
2 tablespoons margarine, softened
2 tablespoons shortening, softened
2 tablespoons oil
About ½ cup cold water

Chocolate Filling

4 cups bittersweet chocolate chips
3 cups soy milk
Pinch salt
2 tablespoons flour

Yields

10 to 12 servings

Working with Crusts

When mixing the crust, the desired consistency is crumbly and tender. When squeezed, the dough should hold together. If it feels too dry and doesn't stick together, add a bit more water. However, be careful not to add too much water or the dough will become elastic and stretchy.

Ingredients

5 cup soy milk
1½ cup sugar
1 tablespoon vanilla extract
½ vanilla bean
½ teaspoon salt
1 tablespoon fresh lemon juice
1 teaspoon liquid soy lecithin

Classic Vanilla Ice Cream

This is a simple recipe that is easy to follow and great to use as a springboard for more creative flavor combinations. There are plenty of tasty vegan ice creams available at most supermarkets these days; however, making your own can be lots of fun.

Directions

1. Simmer the soy milk, sugar, vanilla extract, vanilla bean, and salt in a medium saucepan over low-medium heat until the sugar is dissolved, about 8 minutes.

2. Remove the vanilla bean, and transfer the hot ingredients to a blender.

3. Split the vanilla beans, remove the seeds, and add the seeds to the ingredients, along with the lemon juice and soy lecithin.

4. Blend for 30 second, then allow the mixture to cool in the refrigerator for at least 20 minutes.

5. Transfer ingredients to an ice cream maker and follow manufacturer's instructions. Store ice cream in an air-tight container in the freezer for up to 2 weeks. You may need to thaw the ice cream and re-spin after a few days to maintain the right texture.

Suggested Variations

To create new flavors, simply adjust the ingredients and follow the basic instructions above.

Vanilla-Bourbon Ice Cream
Replace 2 cups of the soy milk with 2 cups of bourbon.

Toasted Coconut Ice Cream
Replace 5 cups the of soy milk with 5 cups coconut ice cream and add 1/2 cup toasted coconut flakes when blending.

Dark Chocolate Ice Cream
Add 1 cup chocolate chips when simmering, and add 1/4 cup cocoa powder and 1 tablespoon instant coffee when blending.

Mango Ice Cream
Replace 3 cups of the soy milk with only 2 cups of coconut milk. Use lime juice instead of lemon juice, and add the fruit of 2 very ripe mangoes when blending.

Sticky Toffee Pudding

Don't be put off by the British term "pudding." This dessert is a favorite in the UK, which I discovered just recently at the Ebbitt Room in Cape May, New Jersey. It's a very moist cake, sweetened with brown sugar and dates, served oven-warm with a smear of toffee sauce. I've served it at the restaurant with a homemade vanilla-bourbon ice cream. It's absolutely perfect for a late fall or winter dessert. So when you've overdosed on all the baked apple and pumpkin desserts by Thanksgiving, turn to this to make the rest of the winter season a lot sweeter.

Directions

1. Preheat oven to 350 degrees.

2. Line a half-sheet pan with parchment paper (or coat it with margarine and a light dusting of flour).

3. In a large mixing bowl, combine the flour, cinnamon, baking powder, and salt.

4. Heat the water with the dried dates, white and brown sugar, shortening, and margarine.

5. Pulse the heated mixture in a food processor until the dates are broken down into small chunks.

6. Add the pulsed liquid ingredients to the dry ingredients, and stir quickly until combined.

7. Pour the batter into the sheet pan, and bake for 30 minutes, turning halfway through to ensure even baking.

8. Meanwhile, make the toffee by combining all ingredients in a saucepan.

9. Melt the margarine and bring to a boil, allowing it to reduce by half.

10. Remove the cake from the oven and allow to cool for a few minutes before cutting into squares.

11. Serve while still warm, drizzled with lots of toffee sauce on top.

12. Garnish with your favorite ice cream, and a few dried, chopped dates.

Cake Ingredients

3 cups flour
½ tablespoon cinnamon
1 teaspoon baking powder
Pinch salt
2 cups water
1 cup dried, pitted dates
1 cup white sugar
1 cup brown sugar
¼ cup shortening
¼ cup margarine

Toffee Ingredients

4 tablespoons margarine
2 cups brown sugar
1 teaspoon vanilla
½ cup soy milk
½ cup apple cider
½ teaspoon cinnamon

Yields

8 to 12 servings

Ingredients

3 cups chocolate chips
24 big, fresh strawberries with stems
   in tact, if possible

Yields

8 servings

Chocolate Covered Strawberries

Here's an easy, classic preparation that can be very versatile in the world of desserts. I have served chocolate covered berries and cookies as garnishes for desserts or arranged on trays for big parties. It's simple to learn this technique and allows for lots of creativity. The challenge is finding news ways to flavor the chocolate to complement whatever is being covered.

Directions

1. Have your strawberries (or other fruits or cookies) clean and ready to dip.

2. Line a sheet pan or cookie tray with foil or parchment paper.

3. Using a double boiler, melt 2 cups of the chocolate chips, stirring until the chips are smooth and thoroughly melted.

4. Remove from heat and add the remaining 1 cup of chips to the melted chocolate, a little at a time, and stir.

   Note: The additional chips will melt smoothly into the chocolate while bringing down the temperature.

5. Once all the chips are melted, you are ready to being dipping.

6. By holding the stems or green leaves of the strawberry, carefully dip each one into the chocolate, coating it evenly and allowing excess chocolate to drip off.

7. Transfer the covered strawberry to the lined sheet pan for cooling, and then dip the next strawberry.

8. After dipping all the strawberries, you may add additional textures and flavors while the chocolate is setting, either by sprinkling the toppings on the setting chocolate or by dipping the entire strawberry a second time into the topping.

9. Allow strawberries to cool for at least 20 minutes in the refrigerator before serving. If storing overnight, be sure to use an airtight container.

Suggestions for Flavoring Chocolate

Mexican
- Add 1 tablespoon instant coffee, ¼ teaspoon cinnamon, and a dash chipotle powder to the melting chocolate.
- Dip berries in cocoa powder as chocolate is setting.

Caribbean
- Add ½ cup coconut milk, ½ teaspoon cinnamon, ¼ teaspoon allspice, and ¼ teaspoon clove to the melting chocolate.
- Dip berries in toasted coconut flakes as chocolate is setting.

French
- Add 2 ounces Grand Marnier® and ½ teaspoon fresh orange zest to the melting chocolate.
- Sprinkle berries lightly with dried lavender flowers as chocolate is setting.

Chocolate Covered Strawberries

Cake Ingredients

3 cups flour
2 cups sugar
½ teaspoon cinnamon
1½ teaspoon baking powder
8 tablespoons shortening
8 tablespoons margarine
6 ounces silken tofu
1 cup coconut milk
1 cup whiskey
½ cup chopped walnuts

Hard Icing Ingredients

1 cup whiskey
¼ cup sugar
2 tablespoons margarine
1 teaspoon vanilla extract

Coconut Icing Ingredients

3 cups powdered sugar
¼ cup margarine, softened
1 teaspoon vanilla extract
¼ cup coconut milk
1 cup unsweetened coconut flakes
3 tablespoons cinnamon

Yields

10 to 12 servings

Irish Potato Cake

Growing up, one of my favorite comfort food desserts was my grandmother's whisky cake. Not only was it delicious, but I always loved the idea that I got to have whisky as a kid—even if the alcohol was all baked out. One year, for St. Patrick's Day, I adapted the recipe a bit by topping the cake with a cinnamon-dusted coconut icing. This of course, was in homage to another favorite childhood treat—Irish Potatoes. I was surprised by how many people were unfamiliar with Irish Potatoes and couldn't grasp the concept of an Irish Potato Cake. Regardless of how weird this dessert may sound, it's a crowd pleaser.

Directions

1. Preheat oven to 350 degrees.

2. Coat a 9-inch Bundt® pan with margarine and a light dusting of flour.

3. In a large mixing bowl, combine the flour, sugar, cinnamon, and baking powder.

4. In a blender, combine the shortening, margarine, silken tofu, soy milk, and whiskey until smooth.

5. Add the wet ingredients to the dry ingredients, and stir quickly until combined.

6. Gently fold in the walnuts last.

7. Pour the batter into the Bundt pan and bake for 25 to 30 minutes, turning halfway through to ensure even baking.

8. Meanwhile, combine the hard icing ingredients in a small saucepan and bring it to a boil, allowing it to reduce by a third.

9. Next, make the coconut icing by combining the powdered sugar, margarine, vanilla extract, and soy milk in a food processor until smooth. Then lightly pulse in the coconut flakes.

10. Allow the cake to cool for 15 minutes, then invert onto a wire rack.

11. Pour half of the hard icing on top of the cake and allow to cool another 15 minutes.

12. Invert the cake again, and pour the rest of the icing on the other side of the cake, allowing the cake to cool and icing to harden completely.

13. Spread the coconut icing over the exterior of the cake, and sprinkle the cinnamon evenly over the top.

Everything Cookies

Chocolate chip cookies are an art. Everyone has their favorite brand, a cherished recipe, and the perfect way to eat them. I have built this recipe around the things I love best in a good chocolate chip cookie: a soft center and lightly crisp outside, tons of dark chocolate chips, a few nuts, vanilla, and a few extras that you can't quite put your finger on. I call them "everything cookies" because like everything bagels, I have a hard time limiting all the flavors.

Directions

1. Combine the margarine, shortening, sugars, agave, and molasses in a food processor until smooth.

2. Add the soy milk, vanilla extract, coconut, salt, cinnamon, and 1 cup of the rolled oats and combine again until the oats are broken down evenly.

3. Transfer this mix to a large bowl, and add the remaining ingredients.

4. Combine with your hands until everything is mixed evenly.

5. Cover with plastic wrap and allow to chill for at least 20 minutes in the refrigerator.

6. Preheat oven to 375 degrees.

7. Form the cookie dough into 2-inch round balls (a mechanical ice cream scoop work best) and arrange on a sheet pan lined with parchment paper, allowing a good 2 inches between each cookie.

8. Bake for about 10 to 12 minutes, turning the sheet pan halfway through to ensure even baking.

   Note: Be sure not to overbake the cookies.

Ingredients

½ cup margarine, softened
½ cup shortening, softened
½ cup brown sugar
1 cup white sugar
2 tablespoons agave syrup
2 tablespoons molasses
2 tablespoons soy milk
1 tablespoon vanilla extract
¼ cup shredded coconut
Pinch salt
½ teaspoon cinnamon
2 cups rolled oats
2 cups flour
½ cup toasted macadamia nuts, chopped
1 cup or more chocolate chips

Yields

2 dozen cookies

PISTACHIOS are great for baking. The flavor is fantastic, and the natural green color adds great contrast. If you're shelling your own pistachios, try to find ones with the shells already splitting. Not only will they be easier to open, but these nuts are riper than ones with closed shells.

Pistachio Biscotti

Pistachio Biscotti

Back in college, my roommate's parents went to Italy. When they got back, they were generous enough to bring back some biscotti. It wasn't flavored with any chocolate or funky nuts or herbs; it was simple and delicious. What I remember most was that it was not the dry, super-crisp biscotti served in the US, but more of a tender and oily biscuit that flaked and crumbled. I haven't been able to find them since, though they're on my list for our next trip to Italy.

Directions

1. Preheat oven to 300 degrees.

2. Line a half-sheet pan with parchment paper (or tin foil).

3. In a food processor, combine cream cheese, margarine, sugar, salt, vanilla extract, and lemon zest until smooth.

4. Add the flour to this mixture and combine again.

5. Add the lemon juice and combine again until the dough forms one large ball in the food processor and is still sticky to touch.

6. Transfer the dough to a large mixing bowl and add the chopped pistachios and mix by hand to incorporate.

7. Divide the dough in three parts and form each third into a log shape.

8. Place logs on sheet pan, and bake for about 20 to 25 minutes or until dough begins to turn golden and is no longer sticky to the touch.

9. Remove from oven and let cool for about 15 minutes.

10. Meanwhile, reduce the oven temperature to 225 degrees.

11. Slice each log into about 12 cookies.

12. Turn the cookies on their sides and bake for 10 minutes.

13. Flip the cookies to the other side and bake another 10 minutes.

14. Remove from oven and allow to cool and dry thoroughly before serving. Store in an air-tight container at room temperature for up to 2 weeks.

Ingredients

4 ounces soy cream cheese
6 tablespoons margarine, softened
1 cup sugar
1 teaspoon salt
1 teaspoon vanilla extract
½ tablespoon lemon zest
1 tablespoon fresh lemon juice
2 cups flour
1 cup roasted, shelled pistachios, chopped

Yields

3 dozen biscotti

Ingredients

1 cup warm water
1 pinch sugar
2 tablespoons yeast powder
3 cups all-purpose flour
1 teaspoon fine salt
1 teaspoon pepper
½ cup olive oil
1 tablespoon coarse salt
2 tablespoons fresh rosemary leaves,
   chopped

Yields

4 to 8 servings, depending on use

Rosemary Focaccia

When we knew we were moving the restaurant to Center City Philadelphia, I took on the responsibility of daily bread baker. I wanted to create a recipe that would be easy enough to execute each morning, yet something that would be very special and memorable for our guests. I began experimenting with focaccia recipes and finally created one that I love. We now serve warm strips of focaccia with a garlic and herb dipping oil with each meal.

Focaccia is a simple yeast bread that is most successful when using lots of quality olive oil and coarse salt. If you're using this as a sandwich bread, you may want to keep the recipe simple. However, if you're serving this to accompany a meal, I like to add fresh chopped herbs.

Directions

1. In a small mixing bowl, combine the water, sugar, and yeast.

2. Allow the yeast to activate and begin rising for about 3 minutes.

3. In a larger bowl or an electric mixer, combine the flour, fine salt, pepper, and ¼ cup of the olive oil.

4. Add the yeast mixture to the flour mixture and combine until a nice, smooth dough has formed into a ball.

   Note: The dough ball should be very pliable and slightly sticky to the touch.

5. Transfer the dough to a sheet pan and cover it with a cloth.

6. Put the sheet pan in a warm place that will encourage rising, such as on top of the refrigerator, and allow dough to rise for 20 minutes.

7. Knead the dough again and roll it out to cover the entire surface of the sheet pan.

8. Cover dough again, and allow it to rise for another 20 minutes.

9. Preheat oven to 400 degrees.

10. Brush the risen dough with the remaining olive oil and sprinkle with the coarse salt and chopped rosemary.

11. Bake for about 12 to 15 minutes or until the top is golden brown.

VEGAN WINE

When we first realized we were getting a liquor license in our new location, I jumped at the opportunity to become the sommelier. Granted, I had no formal training and only a mild appreciation for wine, but I believe I held the two most important characteristics when approaching wine: enthusiasm and a good sense of taste. I felt fully confident that, with time and lots of tasting, I would be able to assemble an impressive list of wines to complement our cuisine.

Sounds simple. But there was one little obstacle, and I'm not referring to the process of selecting and stocking wines in adherence with the strict laws of the Pennsylvania Liquor Control Board system. That is another story. I'm referring to the fact that many wines are not considered vegan.

Originally, when first confronted with this fact, I wanted to believe it was a bit of vegan urban legend. What animal products would ever end up in wine? Why would anyone put eggs in wine? This was crazy talk. After digging a tiny bit deeper, I learned the startling reality that certain animal proteins have been revered by winemakers for centuries for their abilities to help remove sediment from fermenting wine during processes referred to as *fining and filtering*. Most commonly used are egg whites, gelatin, isinglass (or fish bladder). Blood was even widely used, before mad cow disease. Who knew?

For weeks, I conducted internet research and read, scouring the globe via email for wineries committed to producing vegan wines. You see, there are alternative fining agents, such as bentonite or clay, that are made of non-animal ingredients. The current trend these days leans toward less-altered styles of winemaking that require no fining or filtering. So it was up to me to find out which of these wines were both of excellent quality and regularly available in the state of Pennsylvania. Little by little, I convinced Seth, Bill, Jenn, Henry, and Joe (my top cabinet of wine reps) that

Kate opening a new bottle of Petite Sirah that was just added to the restaurant's wine list

finding out the vegan status of the wines they sell is a legitimate task. I educated them on what it means for a wine to be considered vegan and how to talk to winemakers about their products. They embraced the idea, and they responded with cases of delicious vegan wine from all over the world.

So now we offer about 75 bottles on our list, ranging from sweet, minerally Riesling from the steep slopes of the Mosel Saar Ruwer in Germany, to the complex cocoa and berries of the tightly planted Pinot Noir grapes from the Mornington Peninsula of Australia, to the heavily extracted power of Russian River Valley Cabernet Sauvignon.

I feel such a sense of accomplishment when I flip through the pages of our wine book. There are so many interesting varietals and blends, each I've come to know personally. Perhaps the most special to me right now are the few we have picked up from the Chaddsford Winery, just about a 45-minute drive south of the city. Owner and winemaker Eric Miller was kind enough to give Rich and me a personalized tour of his winery, complete with barrel tasting! That was an adventure for us—it was early November, after harvest, while still crushing. We got to taste the first-press juice from locally grown Chambourcin grapes in the midday sunshine on a brisk autumn afternoon in Southeastern Pennsylvania. And next year, that bottle will grace our wine rack. Now that's exciting!

What once seemed like an impossible task has become a new passion for me. I share this passion now with Rich when we plan menus and meet winemakers passing through town with wine reps. We seek out boutique wine shops when we travel, where we can purchase small production bottles, and we love to plot stopping points along our soon-approaching tours of California and French wine country. We have always enjoyed wine, beer, and spirits for their ability to complement foods and complete the dining experience. Now, we regard wine as an integral part of a meal, an essential ingredient like that last splash of fresh citrus on grilled spinach or the sprinkle of coarse sea salt on freshly baked focaccia. (Wine is not for cheese alone!) And if my experience thus far has taught me anything, it's that the world of vegan cuisine has everything to gain by being paired with excellent vegan wines. ■

AFTERWORD

I'm looking out of the airplane window, a little sunburned and travel weary, my eyes transfixed on the turquoise heaven of water below this 757 taking us back to San Juan from St. Martin. Island spotting... there they are: Virgin Gorda, Tortola, Vieques, Culebra...life-size travel advertisements. Green chunky mountains, ringed with white wisps of sandy coast catching the lapping sheets of the sweet Caribbean sea are below me. I say it on every plane ride home: "I must get back here as soon as possible."

As I opened this book recounting a gastronomic nightmare on Guadeloupe, I close with incredible food memories of French St. Martin. We ate good there. It helps that Kate is fluent in French. It also helps to have a better understanding of how the French approach their cuisine, and it definitely helps to carry with you the confidence of running a successful full-scale restaurant in a full-scale city. A long journey indeed from my original lunch counter. It is hard to feel anything but gratitude at times like these. So onward we go. I have to get back to the restaurant. Vacation is great, but it is an illusion. My reality, my life, is in my kitchen. We travel to find beauty and inspiration, but we always come home, eager to cook and create, to bring to a plate the new ideas that we have dreamed of over cocktails at sunset.

I really can't wait to touch down in Philly. When you think about it, there is no better place in the world than September in the northeast. The late summer/early autumn vegetables will be in the Sunday Farmers' Market this week, just five blocks from the restaurant. White eggplant, beautiful sweet bell peppers, heirloom tomatoes of every imaginable shape and color, impossibly sweet corn. I can't wait to cook again.

The life of a restaurateur is hard to explain. You may have heard about the hours, the stress, as well as the unpredictability of ingredients, staff, weather, plumbing, electricity— not to mention the occasional nightmare customer or two. The reality goes well beyond that. The reality, in fact, is that you never leave. You think about the restaurant constantly: when you wake up, before you go to sleep, every moment of the day, and yes, even on vacation. Constantly. It is not a lifestyle. It is life.

Sound intimidating? It is. It's overwhelming at times, and I dare say that it's not for everyone. Hopefully, after reading some of our stories that we have collected over the years and tasting some of our food, you can catch a little glimpse of the sense it all makes to us.

☼

Soon, the leaves will turn and fall. The cool autumn rains will bring us back inside as we prepare for the holidays. The planet takes another trip around the sun. Hopefully, on each cycle we are changing, growing, and evolving for the better.

Whether at the restaurant or in the pages of this book, thank you all for spending some time with us on this journey.

Rich and Kate
19° N over the Eastern Caribbean
September 2007

INDEX

Broccoli
 Coconut & red chile, 133
Broth
 Vegetable. *See also* Stock,
  vegetable
Brownies, espresso, 152
Bruschetta, Vietnamese, 86
Burrito, seitan with chipotle sauce,
 117
Butter, vegan, 141

C

Cabbage
 Salad with peanut-orange dressing,
  63
 Thai tofu soup with curry roasted
  peanuts, 45
Cactus salsa, 82
Caesar salad, 59
Cakes
 Irish potato, 160
 Potato-black olive, 88
Calabaza
 Cuban paella, 99
 Puree with roasted cinnamon oil, 37
Canola oil, 25
Caramelized cauliflower in
 Spanish green garlic sauce,
 130
Caribbean
 Caesar salad, 59
 Chocolate covered strawberries,
  159
 Pumpkin, 37

Cauliflower
 & saffron, olives & fennel couscous,
  108
 & white bean puree with truffle oil,
  50
 in Spanish green garlic sauce, 130
 Roasted with citrus rémoulade, 83
Celery root rémoulade, 140
Chervil, 24
Chilaquiles with scrambled tofu &
 vegetarian ground beef, 97
Chile & tomato quinoa, 136
Chipotle
 Sauce, 117
 Sour cream, 73
Chives, 24
Chocolate
 Covered strawberries, 158
  French, 159
  Mexican, 159
  Caribbean, 159
 Espresso brownies, 152
 Ice cream, 156
 Mousse with toasted coconut, 149
 Peanut butter bombs, 148
 Tart, 155
Chopped Greek salad, 61
Chopping, 21
Chowder
 Vegan Key West conch, 47
Cilantro, 24, 46, 64
 Dressing, 64
 Summer cucumber soup with, 46

Cinnamon oil, 37
Citrus, 23, 83
 Rémoulade, 83
Coconut
 & red chile broccoli, 133
 Toasted
  Ice cream, 156
  with chocolate mousse, 149
Common Ingredients
 Savory foods, 24–30
Cookies
 Everything, 161
 Pistachio biscotti, 163
Cooking methods, v, 19–21
Corn & green olive relish, 85
Couscous
 with preserved lemon, almonds &
  Moroccan olives, 138
 with saffron, olives, fennel &
  cauliflower, 108
Crème brûlée, 151
Cuban
 Paella, 99
 Pan-seared tofu with onions &
  mojo, 100
 Seitan meatloaf picadillo, 126
Cucumber
 Salad with Hawaiian ginger
  dressing, 62
 Soup with cilantro & mint, 46
Cumin, 27, 67

Truffle
Creamy vinaigrette, 56
Golden beet slaw, 135
Hummus, 90
Oil, 25, 50
Sour cream, 89
TSP granules, 103
Cioppino with saffron & fennel, 103
Key West conch chowder, 47

V

Vanilla
Bourbon ice cream, 156
Crème brûlée, 151
Ice Cream, 156
Vegan
Béarnaise, 124
Key West conch chowder, 47
Tarragon butter, 141
Wine, 165
Vegetable stock, 29
Vegetarian
Ground beef, 97
Verde tacos, portobella, 105
Vietnamese bruschetta, 86
Vinaigrette
Creamy truffle, 56
Lime, 67
Miso, 144
Pistachio, 68
Vinegar, 30
Balsamic, 30
Rice wine, 30
White wine, 30

W

White
Bean & artichoke dip, 72
Bean & cauliflower puree with
    truffle oil, 50
Pepper, 28
Truffle oil, 25
Wine vinegar, 30
Wine, 30, 165
Red, 113
Working with
Seitan, 17
Tempeh, 18
Tofu, 14

Y

Yellow gazpacho, 48

Z

Zucchini fettuccine, 142

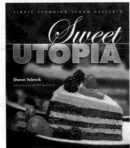